A Sunset Travel Book

National Parks in California

by Dorr Yeager, Former Regional Chief of Interpretation, National Park Service

Second Printing June 1964

L.C. Card: 59-10221. Lithographed in United States of America.
All rights reserved. Second edition. Copyright © 1964, 1959 by

LANE BOOK COMPANY, MENLO PARK, CALIFORNIA

Table of Contents

Cover: M. Litton

How To Enjoy Your National Parks

THIS IS A BOOK ABOUT the national parks of California—Yosemite, Lassen Volcanic, Sequoia, and Kings Canyon. These are but four parks in a system containing 29 and extending from Hawaii to Maine and from Alaska to the Virgin Islands. This system, administered by the National Park Service, is made up not only of national parks, but of national monuments, national battlefields, national military parks, and other areas—over 180 in all—which have been set aside to conserve for all time outstanding scenic, scientific, and historical values that are America's heritage.

It is generally conceded that this new concept of land use was proposed around a campfire at the junction of the Gibbon and the Firehole Rivers in what is now northwestern Wyoming in the year 1870. The Washburn, Langford, Doane Expedition had just completed a superficial exploration of what is now Yellowstone National Park. They had seen enough to confirm the rumors that had been floating into the frontier towns—of hot springs and gushing columns of boiling water and of a great canyon that lay somewhere below the source of the Yellowstone River. On their last night in the region, the proposal was made to convert the wonders they had seen into "a pleasuring ground for the American people." The idea struck fire at once, and less than two years later, on March 1, 1872, President Grant signed the bill creating the world's first national park.

Others followed in rapid succession—Sequoia on September 25, 1890, and Yosemite five days later. What a week for California! She is indeed fortunate, containing not only more national parks than any state in the Union, but the second and third oldest parks as well.

Until 1916, the administration of the national parks and monuments was complicated by the fact that no bureau had ever been established to handle the rapidly growing system. The parks had been supervised by military superintendents and civilian superintendents, and the army had patrolled the areas as best it could. By 1916, however, there had been created sixteen national parks and twenty-one national monuments which were being administered by the Department of the Interior. In that year the National Park Service was established ". . . to conserve the scenery and the natural and historic objects and the wildlife therein, and to provide for the enjoyment of the same in such a manner and by such means as will leave them unimpaired for the enjoyment of future generations."

This same general philosophy had been written into the act of March 1, 1872 that created Yellowstone, which made mandatory "the preservation from injury and spoilation of all timber, mineral deposits, natural curiosities, or wonders within said park, and their retention in their natural condition . . ." In addition, it protected all wildlife against "wanton destruction" and "capture or destruction for the purpose of merchandise or profit."

The wisdom of the far-sighted men who framed that early legislation becomes more apparent as the years pass. Through it, America is now assured that some of her virgin forests will be spared, that some of her waterfalls will never be harnessed for power, that some of her mountains will never be desecrated by mine shafts and slag dumps, that some of her spots where history was born will not be used for agricultural or industrial purposes, and that some of her treasures of antiquity will not be dug up by vandals. In a word, these areas are administered in such a manner that everything within the boundaries remains in a natural condition. This is not only the guiding policy of the Park Service but a mandate from the Congress as well. Some exceptions must be made, of course, in order that the areas may be made accessible to visitors. Roads and trails are constructed, and accommodations provided; but each such intrusion is given careful scrutiny by experts of the National Park Service who see that a minimum of harm is done to the natural values of the area involved.

Not only are the features of a national park jealously guarded, but the precedent is rigidly adhered to of admitting only outstanding examples as a part of the system. There is but one Yosemite, and to establish another national park of lesser grandeur but of the same general characteristics would be to lower the high standards which have been established. Nowhere else is there a Yellowstone or a McKinley or a Sequoia.

Many people are confused by the difference between the National Park Service and the United States Forest Service. The former is administered by the Department of the Interior, and the latter is a bureau of the Department of Agriculture. Both are conservation agencies, but

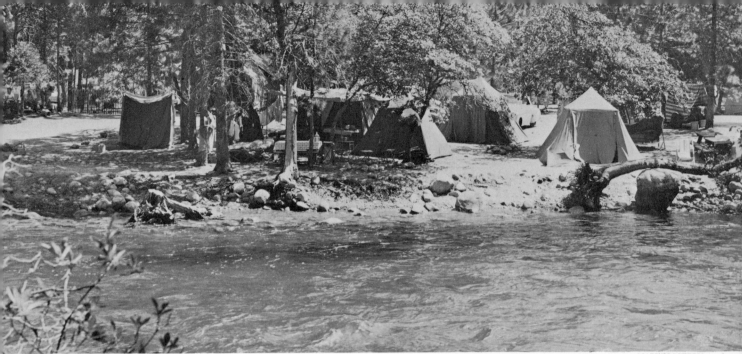

Scenic and recreational attractions *of Yosemite Valley draw many campers, particularly in these choice sites along river*

the Forest Service scientifically "harvests" its crops of trees, leases its mountain meadows for cattle and sheep grazing, and permits mining and hunting. None of these activities is carried on in a national park, although there is always pressure from commercial interests to open the parks for such uses.

Heading the National Park Service is a Director who, with his staff in Washington, administers a far-flung empire consisting of five regions with headquarters in Richmond, Philadelphia, Omaha, Santa Fe, and San Francisco. Each region is administered by a Regional Director who is the Director's representative in dealing with the areas under his direction. A national park is headed by a Superintendent assisted by an Assistant Superintendent, Chief Park Ranger, Chief Park Naturalist, Chief Engineer, and other department heads.

A word of advice about what is termed "a national park experience." National parks are to be enjoyed in any way which does not lessen their value to the American people. Here one finds opportunity for unique experiences, for mental and physical relaxation, and for spiritual re-creation. When you visit a park, plan to do things you cannot do at home—otherwise, why go? There are unlimited opportunities for visitors to fish and hike, to camp and to "climb the mountains and get their good tidings" as John Muir said.

General Information

Plan Your Trip: Too often, visitors return from a national park only to discover from friends who were pre-

viously there that they missed much that was worth while. Or they arrive in a park completely ignorant of what it has to offer and spend valuable time learning what to see instead of seeing it. All of which adds up to the value of planning a trip to get the most out of it. This book will help you do that. In addition, read other books and write the Superintendent of the park for free government literature. The National Park Service maintains an information desk at its regional office, 180 New Montgomery St., San Francisco, where you can ask questions and obtain all sorts of information. Map out your trip according to the time you have to spend. Once at the park, go to the Superintendent's office or the museum and talk with the man on duty. He will be more than glad to help you.

What to Wear: Outdoor clothes are in vogue in a national park, but your wardrobe will depend upon what kind of vacation you plan. Needless to say, if you do not intend to do any hiking, you will not need jeans and good walking shoes. If you plan to spend most of your time lounging around lodges and hotels, ordinary sport outfits are appropriate, but it is hoped that you will do more than this. High heels are out except for dinner and dancing—so are "evening clothes." It can be chilly after the sun goes down, and you will welcome a coat or sweater. On the other hand, days can be hot, especially in Yosemite Valley and at Cedar Grove in Kings Canyon. Women will probably see more of their sex in slacks, pedal pushers, and shorts than in dresses during the day. But again, let your activities dictate your wardrobe.

When to Go: You will find crowds from July 1st to Labor Day, especially on weekends. More and more people are discovering the many advantages of going before and after those dates if possible. Accommodations are less crowded, the weather is delightful, and most of the mid-summer activities are available before and after "the season."

Learn About the Area: Take advantage of the free government programs—talks, museums, guided trips afield, and sometimes auto caravans. Through these you will really learn about your park and better enjoy it. Consult the schedules of such activities, posted conspicuously throughout the areas, or inquire at the lodges or from anyone in uniform.

Rangers Are Your Friends: You will find the rangers friendly and helpful. Although the ranger service has full police powers, it prides itself on making few arrests. The park staff wants you to enjoy the area to the fullest and goes out of its way to help you do so. National Park Service employees (and you will know them by the forest green uniform and the stiff-brimmed Stetson) are men devoted to an ideal. The permanent staff is augmented in summer by a large number of temporary rangers and ranger naturalists, mostly teachers and graduate students, who are carefully screened and selected for their personalities and skill in handling people. One thing you should remember—they are busy men, and questions which are "thought up" simply for an opening to chat are quickly spotted. If you are in trouble or need information or advice, ask the man in forest green.

Concessioners: All hotels, lodges, stores, etc., in a national park are concessions under contract with the Department of the Interior. The National Park Service approves rates, inspects facilities for cleanliness and sanitation, and will be glad to know of any cases of discourtesy on the part of concession employees. You will find the rates reasonable, especially when you consider the long distances from railroads and the fact that in such parks as Lassen Volcanic, where snow removal is a real problem, the concessioner must carry his heavy overhead and make a fair profit within the few months that he is open.

Don't Feed the Animals: You'll see others doing it but don't let it tempt you. It is not only against regulations, but it is dangerous to feed bears and deer, and if you persist you may regret it. Hundreds of people are injured by this practice; so don't take chances. Deer look like timid, docile creatures, but they may strike suddenly with their sharp front hoofs for no apparent reason. Also there is an old saying that "it's a wise bear that knows where the candy leaves off and the fingers begin."

Be Careful With Fire: This slogan has been so publicized by state and federal agencies and by private organizations that there should be no need to repeat it here.

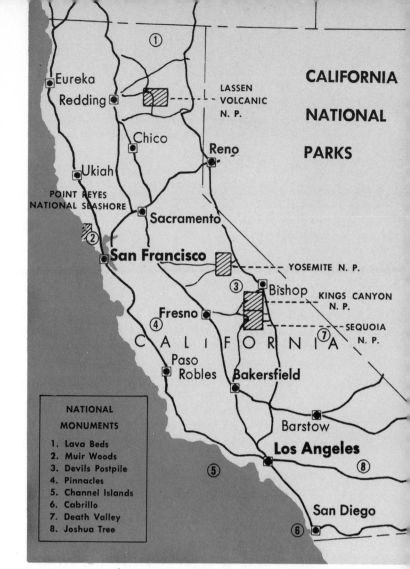

Yet the majority of serious fires are still man-caused. Be sure your fire is dead before leaving it. Don't throw burning material from your car. It is best not to smoke at all while traveling through the parks.

Don't Be a Litterbug: Gum wrappers, film cartons, and beer cans have never enhanced the landscape. Once a National Park Service man ruefully observed that "Kleenex is rapidly becoming the national flower" and one has but to look along the roadside to see the truth of his observation. Carry a paper bag in your car, and when it is full, deposit it in a garbage container. Some parks provide such bags at the entrance.

Entrance Fees: Nominal park entrance fees are charged for automobiles, motorcycles, and trailers. One can obtain a short term or an annual permit at the park entrance. Fees collected are primarily for the use of park roads, but such collections do not revert to the park for its use. Instead, they are turned in to the Treasury of the United States. All funds for running and maintaining a national park are a direct appropriation by the Congress.

Pets: Leave your pets at home—they will have a better time, since all pets must be kept on leash or under physical restraint. Kennels are available in some areas (see under specific area), but if at all possible enjoy a "petless vacation."

Children: Keep an eye on the kids. Rangers waste many hours looking for lost children. In summer, Yosemite Valley at times accommodates more than 33,000 persons in an area of four square miles. In such a crowd it is easy enough for a child to become confused in his directions.

Take it Easy: Most parks are at a higher altitude than that to which you are accustomed; so break yourself in gradually and don't try to climb a mountain the first day. Even though your legs stand it, your heart may not.

Don't Pick the Flowers: This admonition should not be needed any more than "Be Careful With Fire." Flowers, shrubs, and trees are all part of the natural scene. Leave them for others to enjoy.

Make Reservations Early: This cannot be stressed too strongly. Often lodges and hotels are booked months in advance, so get your order in early. However, if you make a late decision to take your vacation in a national park, do not hesitate to write for accommodations, because there are often openings or cancellations available, particularly for the month of August. If you are camping, no reservations are required, but you should arrive soon enough in the day to be sure you get a site.

Planning A High Country Vacation

This section is written for the ever-increasing number who wish to get away from the paved roads and hit the trails into the back country. Whether you wish to go only overnight or to spend a week or a month, you will probably find something that is helpful in these paragraphs. The following tips are not for those who are trail wise, but rather for those who have never been into the High Country and feel that they would like a new experience. What is said applies largely to Yosemite, Sequoia, and Kings Canyon, since most of the back country travel occurs in these parks; but there is also ample opportunity for hiking in Lassen Volcanic.

First of all, there are the backpackers, who go where they please, unhampered by horses or mules. Generally, they carry packs that range from thirty to fifty pounds (less for a woman), depending upon the ruggedness of the individual and how much in the way of comfort he is willing to forego. This is the cheapest kind of a vacation and permits one to get into sections inaccessible to

pack stock. This type of back country travel tests your ingenuity in selecting items that weigh the least, such as dehydrated foods, and in making one piece of equipment serve several purposes to make a lighter pack. More and more items designed especially for the backpacker are appearing on the market—light but warm sleeping bags, light pack frames, featherweight cooking utensils, and above all, light and nourishing food. The presence of one-year-olds need not deter you from a backpacking trip. Many are taken along papoose-fashion and enjoy it.

The next cheapest method is to walk and lead a burro that carries the load. The company of this patient beast enables you to take along a few more luxuries than the backpacker can carry. You do not have to depend so much on dried and concentrated foods, and you can take a few cans to liven up the menu. The extra carrying capacity also enables you to have a more frequent change of clothing and possibly a light nylon tent in case of rain. There *are* disadvantages, however, in that a burro must be fed, watered, and occasionally cajoled when there is not a meeting of minds.

You can also rent riding horses and pack stock, but unless you have had experience in packing, and unless you are willing to get up early and frequently spend several chilly hours chasing stock that has wandered away, this method is not recommended for your first trip.

Another way, which is especially popular in Sequoia and Kings Canyon, particularly with family groups that like to "stay put," is known as "spotting in." Here you ride or walk to a predetermined campsite where a packer meets you with all your equipment and supplies. He leaves you for as long as you wish to stay and returns on a definite date, either to set you down at another campsite farther on or to take you back to your starting point. A two or three-week vacation "spotted in" is an inexpensive venture. A packer and his horse cost about $20 a day. If you can limit your dunnage and food to 150 pounds, one pack animal can carry it, and that will cost you another $6 to $8. If you are out for very long, however, you should figure on 300 pounds. For example, if you select a spot to camp where the packer can get in and out in a day, and if you have 300 pounds of equipment but elect to hike in, the cost will be $40 to take your supplies and equipment in and the same amount to come and get you on the date you select. If you would rather ride with the packer, a horse will cost you $6 to $8 each way.

Finally, there is the deluxe method, which subjects you to a minimum of discomfort and physical exertion. This is the regular pack trip where all the worries are shifted to the guide. He will make suggestions as to an itinerary or will follow one you have selected if it is within reason. He handles the horses, the packing, the wood gathering, the fire building, and even the cooking. Naturally, this is a relatively expensive vacation, but there is no question that the packer earns his wages, even though members of the party may help with certain of the camp chores.

It is suggested that before settling on any of the above methods of travel, you invest two dollars and purchase a copy of *Going Light with Backpack or Burro,* published by the Sierra Club, Mills Tower, San Francisco. It is an excellent book with all kinds of hints on High Country travel and living.

What to wear and how to live are subjects upon which there is no complete agreement and where individual likes and dislikes play an important part. There are certain cardinal rules, however, with which most people concur.

First of all, don't push yourself, especially if you decide to backpack. Mountain sickness due to overexertion is no fun, and sometimes it is better to have no destination at all than to wear yourself out getting there. If you are backpacking, don't take too big a load. Remember that a load that seems light in the living room of your home before departure is a lot heavier at the top of a 12,000-foot pass. Unless you are able to sleep comfortably without one, get a light air mattress. A full-sized one is not essential. To save weight, investigate the sectional types which come in 18-inch squares that snap together. One section will cushion the hips, and that may be all you need. If you are in timbered country, you can use pine needles in lieu of a mattress. They remain fairly soft for one night, and if you are spending a second night, they can be "fluffed up." *Don't* try making a bough mattress. Cutting branches is against park regulations, and the bough mattress is liable to be painfully uncomfortable anyway.

Spend more time figuring out what you don't need than what you do need. Here are some essentials—dark glasses, small first aid kit, sunburn lotion, insect repellent, several long leather thongs, pocket knife, and a topographic map. A snake-bite kit is also desirable as there are rattlers in certain sections. If you are a fisherman and want to take a limit back home, take along enough salt to preserve your catch. If you rub salt on the fish right after cleaning, they will keep for several days. Hang them up to cool at night, and wrap them in a sleeping bag during the heat of the day.

As for clothing—good sturdy footwear is essential. The battle between granite and shoes is never-ending, and unless you are properly soled, the granite will always win. Wear shoes (not boots) that are light and strong, and that are soled with thick composition. Composition soles assure better footing on rocks than do leather ones, but some are slippery on wet surfaces. Don't buy a pair of hiking shoes and start out the next day. Wear them around home until they are thoroughly broken in. Buy ankle-high shoes that are large enough to accommodate your foot plus one or more pairs of soft wool socks and, if you prefer, a pair of silk or nylon ones underneath. For trousers, select a material that is strong but not heavy. Before you get back, the seat may show the result of sitting and sliding on rocks. Jeans are popular with both men and women. Many hikers remove the cuffs so they won't be tripped by an outcropping or a dead branch. A pair of light slippers or moccasins for camp wear after a day's hike are most welcome. Cotton shirts are good for daytime wear, but take a wool one plus a sweater or light jacket for early morning and evening. Rain gear of some sort is needed, because you will probably have a shower or two before you return. Some people prefer a light nylon parka, while others like a full-length raincoat. A poncho or a light ground cloth may also be used and can double as a shelter and windbreak.

Another item which you should never be without is a topographic map of the park you plan to visit. Learn to read it and you will always know the kind of country you are going into. It is a must not only for planning but for executing your trip. You will also find *Starr's Guide to the John Muir Trail and the High Sierra Region* most helpful. This book, published by The Sierra Club, Mills Tower, San Francisco, contains a wealth of information on routes, mileages, and what kind of trails you are liable to encounter. It costs only two dollars and covers the three southernmost parks—not Lassen.

The litterbug menace is even more serious in the High Country than it is along the park roads because of the difficulty of disposing of cans and bottles. Many slogans have been adopted in an effort to curb the litterbug habit, but the following should suffice for any thinking person—"Let no one say, and to your shame, that all was beauty here until you came."

Clean your campsite before leaving. Burn empty cans to get rid of odors, then flatten and bury them. Drown your fire and then cover it with mineral soil—not duff or other inflamable material. Leave the site in such a condition that the next party will want to stop there. As far as latrines go, it probably isn't necessary to dig one unless you plan to spend several days in one spot. However, "always emulate.the cat."

Yosemite National Park

World-famous Half Dome *dominates the upper end of Yosemite Valley, rising 4,800 feet above the Valley floor. Note The Ahwahnee hotel nestled in trees at base of cliffs*

PHOTO BY MARTIN LITTON

How to Get There

By Car: The park is reached from the north via Manteca over State 120 or from Merced over State 140. From Southern California you can take State 41 from Fresno, or you can enter from Leevining on the east side over the steep 9-mile grade to Tioga Pass. The Fresno and Merced routes are the only ones open the year around, and they are also less steep than the other two. The distance from Merced to the Valley is 81 miles and from Fresno 94 miles.

By Train, Bus, and Air: Santa Fe and Southern Pacific trains as well as Greyhound and Continental Trailway buses serve Fresno and Merced. The Yosemite Transportation System runs its buses from Merced to the park throughout the year, and from Fresno and Lake Tahoe during the summer season.

Merced is served by United Air Lines and Fresno by both United and T.W.A.

Where to Stay

In Yosemite you can find practically any type of accommodation you wish. It is advisable to make reservations well in advance of your visit, particularly if you plan to stay in the Valley. However, if you should make a spur-of-the-moment decision to visit Yosemite, don't hesitate to write for accommodations, as there are sometimes openings or last-minute cancellations. Accommodations without bath are often obtainable on short notice. The outlying spots such as Glacier Point, Wawona, and Big Trees Lodge are not so in demand, but even here, make your reservations as far in advance as possible.

The Ahwahnee is undoubtedly one of the most luxurious hotels in any of the national parks. Even though you do not stay there, you should at least visit in and walk through the spacious lobby and the great lounge. If you feel in an expansive mood, have a dinner there. American plan rates for two with bath begin at $20 each, either in the main building or in attractive cottages. The grounds are beautifully landscaped, and there are tennis courts as well as a small golf course. Closed mid-November to Christmas.

Yosemite Lodge offers a variey of sleeping accommodations from attractive motel-type units with radiant heat to canvas-walled cabins. The central portion of the modern lodge contains a cafeteria, restaurant, lounge, writing room, souvenir shop, and cocktail lounge. The most expensive accommodations (without meals) are $14 for two in a room and are graduated to about $5.50 for two in tent cabins, with several steps in between. Meals are good and, at the cafeteria, are probably cheaper than comparable city meals. Open all year.

Camp Curry facilities and accommodations are a little more rustic in nature. Rates are approximately the same as at Yosemite Lodge. Camp Curry operates on European or American plan. The central buildings contain a cafeteria, restaurant, souvenirs, and writing room. It is much older than the Lodge, but a favorite of many. Limited operations during off-season.

Glacier Point Hotel on the rim 3,214 feet above the Valley offers the finest views of any hostelry in Yosemite. Although the main building was constructed in 1917, the adjoining Mountain House is history itself—a real old timer built in 1878. The cafeteria is located in this building, as are a limited number of lower priced rooms. Rates in the hotel, two in a room, are $6.50 each (with bath); and in the Mountain House $3.50 each for two. It is worthwhile to spend at least one night here, if only to watch the firefall being pushed over the cliff. Open from approximately June 1 to mid-September.

Wawona Hotel. It is a treat to stop at the Wawona, which with its big trees and spacious lawns retains all the graciousness and atmosphere of the 70's when it was constructed. It is located a few miles from the South Entrance to the park, and 27 miles from Yosemite Valley on the road to the Mariposa Grove of giant sequoias. Here you will find tennis, stables, a swimming pool, and a beautiful 9-hole golf course of 3,035 yards. The rates are American plan and are comparable to the Lodge and Camp Curry—two in a room with connecting bath, $14 each. Rooms with private baths are correspondingly more and those without bath less. Open from mid-June to about September 1.

Big Trees Lodge is located in the heart of the Mariposa Grove, 36 miles from Yosemite Valley, 5 miles from the South Entrance (State 41). This is a delightful spot with fewer people than at any of the above places. Rates for two in a room are $6.50 each (with bath), European plan. Food at the cafeteria is good. If you wish, you can take your tray outside and eat on the patio under the trees.

White Wolf Lodge is 31 miles from Yosemite Valley on the Tioga Road. The entrance road turns left 14 miles beyond Crane Flat. It's an informal place with either tent or cabin accommodations which, although rustic, are quite comfortable. Horses are available and, within a short distance, you can get to some good fishing. Rates range from $3.50 per person in a tent to $10 in a cabin with private bath. Meals are reasonably priced. Elevation is 8,000 feet. Open from mid-June to about September 1.

Tuolumne Meadows Lodge is the only one of the High Sierra Camps that is accessible by car. It is 55 miles from Yosemite Valley and 12 miles from Tioga Pass. The Tuolumne Meadows section is one of the most beautiful in the whole park, and many people return year after year because of the possibilities for hiking and fishing. This is a *camp* not a lodge. You sleep under canvas and eat under canvas and the meals are served family style. Rates for two in a tent are $3.50 each. Breakfast and lunch are $1.50 and dinner is $3.

The High Sierra Camps are a series of camps in the High Country spaced at easy hiking or riding distance from one another on a 52-mile trail loop that takes about a week to cover on foot. Accommodations and rates for all camps are the same as at Tuolumne Meadows. For more information on these camps, see the section "Yosemite Regions and What To Do in Each." The camps are open from late June to early September.

Free Government Campgrounds are well distributed throughout the park. There are twenty in all, and combined they provide 3,876 campsites. All campgrounds on the Valley floor are large; one (Camp 14) contains 800 camps. Valley campgrounds are more crowded and hotter in summer than those in the outlying areas. All have flush toilets, tap water, a limited number of tables and benches, garbage collection, and space for trailers (except Camp 15). Camp 15 is the only one with fireplaces. Wood may be purchased from the concessioner at the Housekeeping Camp, or you are permitted to use dead, fallen wood throughout the park *except* in the sequoia groves. Because of the crowded conditions in the Valley in summer, more and more people are learning the advantages of using the outlying campgrounds. Most of these are smaller and have few conveniences (pit instead of flush toilets), but they are generally less dusty and are cooler and more pleasant. These campgrounds are located as follows: two adjacent to Big Oak Flat Road—Carl Inn and Crane Flat (new); eight on or adjacent to Tioga Pass Road—Tamarack Flat, Smokey Jack, White Wolf, Harden Lake, Yosemite Creek, Tenaya Lake, Porcupine Flat, Tuolumne Mea-

YOSEMITE FACTUAL INFORMATION

dows; two on the Glacier Point Road—Bridalveil Creek and Glacier Point; one on the Wawona Road about a mile west of Wawona Hotel.

The campgrounds in the Valley are open from about mid-May to mid-September, except Camp 4 which may be used the year around. Snow conditions govern the opening of outlying campgrounds, but most of them are ready from sometime the latter part of May to July 1 and close in September and October. Several of those mentioned above are being improved under the Park Service's Mission 66 program. Most of the larger campgrounds in the park have a registration booth. You should register. This is for your own convenience in case emergency messages arrive during your stay.

Because of increasing use of the park campgrounds, it has been necessary to place certain time limits on camping. During June, July, and August, limits are as follows: 10 days for all Yosemite Valley campgrounds; 14 days for campgrounds at Wawona, Bridalveil Creek, Tenaya Lake, and Tuolumne Meadows.

Choice campsites are, naturally, in great demand, and it is advisable to arrive at the campground early in the day to select your campsite.

Housekeeping Camp: The Yosemite Park and Curry Co. operates housekeeping facilities on the floor of the Valley. Cabins with or without bath are available the year around and tent-cabins are available in summer. The main Housekeeping Camp and an annex are near Camp Curry. Rates vary according to the amount of housekeeping equipment you are going to need. A completely furnished tent for example is $5 for one or two persons and $1.50 for each additional person. A substantial discount is given on weekly rates.

Facilities Available

Stores, etc.: You will find ample facilities for shopping in Yosemite. A large general store is operated in the Valley all year, and a Wawona store and smaller stores at Camp 14 and at Housekeeping Camp are open during the summer. Groceries may also be obtained at Tuolumne Meadows in summer. Ice is available during the summer at Yosemite Village, Housekeeping Camp, Camp 14, and at Wawona. Some groceries are available at White Wolf.

Meals can be obtained at Degnan's and the Village Coffee Shop; at Yosemite Lodge, Camp Curry, and The Ahwahnee; at Wawona, Big Trees, Glacier Point, White Wolf, and Tuolumne Meadows.

Best's Studio in the Valley has a large supply of photographic materials, as well as souvenirs, books, enlargements, etc. It also is open the year around as are the shops and studios in The Ahwahnee and Yosemite Lodge. Camp Curry, Glacier Point, Wawona, and Mariposa Grove have shops and studios that are open during the summer season.

Hospital, Medical, and Dental: The Lewis Memorial Hospital in the Valley is open the year around with a complete staff of doctors and nurses. Dental service is also available. In addition, during the ski season a first aid station is maintained at the Badger Pass ski area.

Churches: Weekly service for most denominations are held during the summer. In winter there are both Protestant and Catholic services in the community chapel, another historical landmark (1879) in the Valley.

Service Clubs: Yosemite has its own chapter of Lions International that meets at noon the first and third Thursdays of each month at The Ahwahnee. Several other service clubs are available in Merced.

Transportation Within the Park: Bus tours can be taken throughout the Valley and to most of the outlying areas. Taxi service is available in the Valley itself.

Baby Sitting can be arranged at Camp Curry, Yosemite Lodge, The Ahwahnee, and Wawona Hotel. Also, in summer, there are the Kiddy Kamp and the Grizzly Club for young campers, and the National Park Service offers a Junior Ranger Program which is excellent for youngsters spending a few days in the Valley.

Laundry and dry cleaning are handled in the Valley through the store. Self-service laundry is also available.

Pets can be brought to the park but must be kept under physical control at all times. Boarding kennels are available within the park. Campers with dogs or cats are required to camp in Camp 4 in the Valley or at special campsites. Cats and dogs are not allowed on trails or in public buildings.

Gas, Oil, and Repairs: Gas and oil as well as towing service are to be found throughout the park. There is a well-equipped garage and repair service in the Valley.

Mail: The main post office is in the Valley and is open throughout the year as are offices at Wawona and Yosemite Lodge. Additional summer post offices are located at Tuolumne Meadows and Camp Curry. Letters addressed c/o General Delivery will arrive at the main post office, or they can be addressed to you at the lodging unit in which you are staying—for example, Glacier Point Hotel, Yosemite National Park, California.

Telephone and Telegraph: There are pay phones throughout the park and telegraph service in summer.

Automobile Clubs: The California State Automobile Association (an affiliate of A.A.A.) maintains a representative in the lobby of the Superintendent's Office at Yosemite Village throughout the summer. There is no N.A.C. representative, but the company garage in the Valley honors calls from N.A.C. members.

Swimming is enjoyed in pools at both Yosemite Lodge and Camp Curry, and there is a small pool located at the Wawona Hotel. Sections of the Merced River are popular swimming areas, although the water is cold.

Bicycling is an easy way to get around the Valley and the roads are ideal for this sport. You can rent bicycles at a nominal fee either at Yosemite Lodge, Camp Curry, and the Housekeeping Camp.

Horses can be rented from the Yosemite Stables at the rate of $3 for two hours, including a guide. Riding stables are also located at Tuolumne Meadows, Wawona, and White Wolf.

Tennis and Golf: There are two golf courses: a small one at The Ahwahnee and a large one (9 holes, 3,035 yards) at Wawona. Both hotels also have tennis courts.

Dancing during the summer season is enjoyed nightly except Sunday at The Ahwahnee. You need not be a guest to attend. During the winter, dancing is offered at The Ahwahnee and Yosemite Lodge.

Fishing

There *are* fish in the Merced River, especially from the lower end of the Valley to the park boundary. If you are an expert you can get them on the floor of the Valley, but if not you will probably have better luck from Valley View downstream. There are plenty of fish in the back country away from the roads and, of course, the farther you go, the better the fishing. As in the other parks, you would be wise to consult the rangers as to just where and when to fish, for they are well informed about seasonal conditions. A California license is required and can be purchased at most of the stores in the park. Seasons correspond to the state season, and the limit is 10 fish or 10 pounds and one fish.

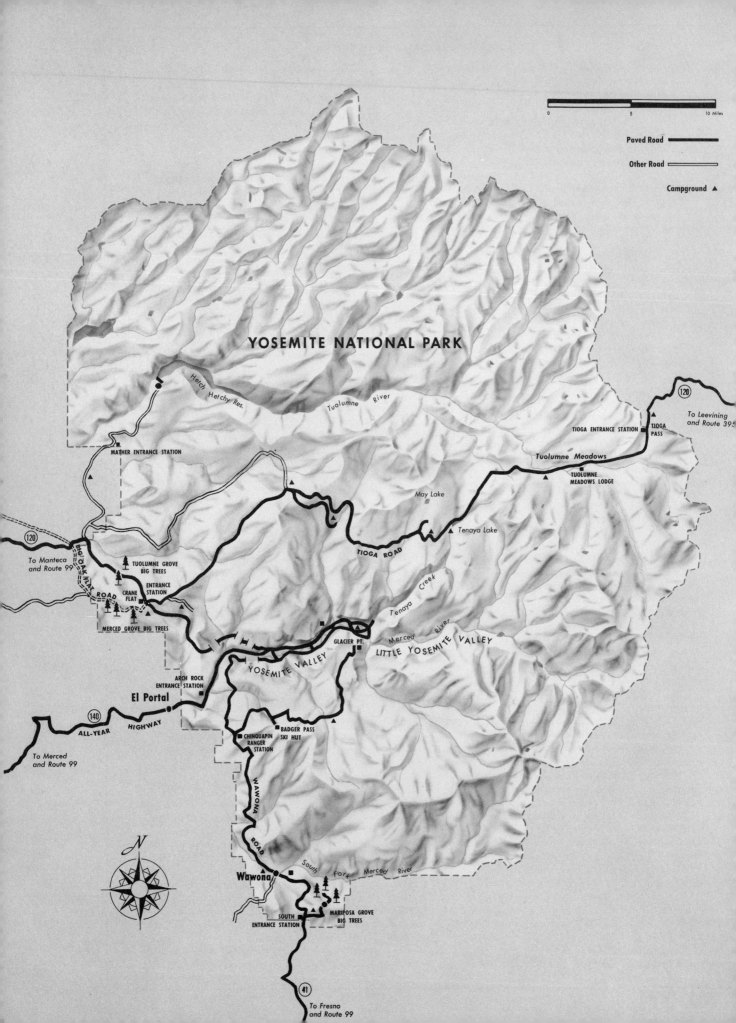

YOSEMITE NATIONAL PARK

Paved Road
Other Road
Campground ▲

0   5   10 Miles

Hetch Hetchy Res.

Tuolumne River

120
To Leevining
and Route 395

MATHER ENTRANCE STATION

TIOGA ENTRANCE STATION   TIOGA
PASS

Tuolumne Meadows

TUOLUMNE
MEADOWS LODGE

May Lake

120
To Manteca
and Route 99

BIG OAK FLAT ROAD

TUOLUMNE GROVE
BIG TREES

Tenaya Lake

TIOGA ROAD

ENTRANCE
STATION
CRANE FLAT

Tenaya Creek

MERCED GROVE BIG TREES

Merced River

YOSEMITE VALLEY

LITTLE YOSEMITE VALLEY

GLACIER PT.

ARCH ROCK
ENTRANCE STATION

El Portal

140
ALL-YEAR   HIGHWAY

BADGER PASS
SKI HUT

CHINQUAPIN
RANGER
STATION

To Merced
and Route 99

WAWONA   ROAD

South   Fork   Merced   River

Wawona

SOUTH
ENTRANCE STATION

MARIPOSA GROVE
BIG TREES

N

41
To Fresno
and Route 99

BY ANY STANDARD, YOSEMITE IS one of the most beautiful national parks in the system. There is beauty of form in the graceful domes and towering cliffs, there is beauty of motion in the spray of its plunging waterfalls, and there is beauty of color from the snow-white dogwoods that border the Merced River to the purple glow on the canyon walls at sunset.

Californians know Yosemite, and they are as proud of it as they are of the Golden Gate or the giant sequoias, but it is a little surprising to find many travelers from east of the Mississippi who are unfamiliar with or even who have never heard of this great national park.

Yosemite contains approximately 1,200 square miles, of which only 7 are taken up by the famous Valley. All too few of the million people who annually visit the park go beyond the confines of the Valley itself—which is another way of saying that all too few visitors really see Yosemite National Park. There is no question but that the Valley is the park's greatest scenic attraction with its thundering waterfalls, its carved granite domes, and its walls that rise 3,000 feet on either side. But there are other attractions—glaciers, giant sequoias, Alpine meadows and 13,000-foot Sierra Nevada peaks. So go to Yosemite with the knowledge that all the beauty and wonder of this great park is not concentrated in 7 square miles, even though many of the accommodations and most of the people are found there.

Yosemite is California's most popular park and one of the most popular in the nation. In the first place, it is only four or five hours by car from the San Francisco Bay area and a little over 300 miles from Los Angeles. It offers an exceptionally wide variety of accommodations ranging from free, government campgrounds to the beautiful and luxurious Ahwahnee hotel. It has an equally wide variety of "things to do"—hiking, bicycling, horseback riding, swimming, fishing, camping, tennis, and even golf. Some of these activities may not contribute to the visitors' "national park experience" but they *do* contribute to the ever-increasing popularity of Yosemite. In addition, the park is open twelve months of the year and each season has its own particular charm.

This may be the place to mention something that irritates those who have known Yosemite for many years —and to offer advice which may save you a disappointment. One occasionally hears the statement, "I'll never go back to Yosemite—it's too crowded." Most of those who make this statement are not speaking of Yosemite National Park as a whole, but of the 7 square miles of Yosemite Valley. In summer the Valley *is* crowded. During this season it is a small city which has contained more than 33,000 individuals on holidays and about 15,000 a night

Yosemite Falls *is composed of three separate parts, one of which is over eight times the height of Niagara. In the spring, its thundering roar can be heard throughout Valley*

on many weekends. Why do people go to Yosemite and stay in the Valley, where they find, except for the scenery, urban conditions similar to those in their own home comunity? Perhaps it is because many of them are not aware of the charm of some of the outlying areas of the park, and then again it may be that "people like to be where people are." The point is, when making plans for a Yosemite visit, don't overlook the advantages of staying at such places as Big Trees Lodge, White Wolf, Wawona, Glacier Point, or Tuolumne Meadows.

There are advantages also in visiting Yosemite during the "off seasons," especially in May and early June and after Labor Day. You will find a different Yosemite then.

Yosemite Valley *as seen from above the Wawona Road Tunnel. El Capitan rises 3,604 feet above floor of the Val-* *ley at the left; Clouds Rest and Half Dome appear in distance; Cathedral Rocks and Bridalveil Fall are at the right*

The park is uncrowded and quiet, Nature seems at her best, and most of the accommodations available in summer are open.

History

It is possible that the first white man saw Yosemite as early as 1833 when Captain Joseph Walker crossed the Sierra and described a country that bears a striking resemblance to the present park area. A later description, which leaves little doubt that it was Yosemite Valley, was given by William Abrams who, in 1849, became lost while tracking a bear. Apparently the first white men ever to enter the Valley were members of the Mariposa Battalion headed by Major James D. Savage. This expedition in 1851 had a single purpose—to capture a group of Indians living in the Valley in retaliation .for raids on the encroaching settlers. The Indians, who called themselves "U-zu-ma-ti" (grizzly bear), were led by a chief named Tenaya. The expedition failed in its purpose but it did accomplish two things. It captured one sick Indian, and

it discovered a valley that was to become world famous.

In 1855, James Hutchings, guided by two Indians, brought in the first group of "tourists." Hutchings was Yosemite's first publicity agent, for upon his return he began writing and publishing articles about its beauty. The Valley soon became the objective of many who were physically capable of making the strenuous trip. Many influential persons visited the area and presently the idea gained momentum that the area should be set aside to protect it from exploitation. In 1864, President Lincoln signed an act providing that the area be granted to California for "public use, resort and recreation." This was eight years before the famous campfire at the junction of the Gibbon and Firehole rivers which resulted in the creation of Yellowstone as the world's first national park. So, while Yosemite was not the first of the parks, the idea which led ultimately to its national status was conceived before that of Yellowstone.

The first "guardian" of Yosemite was Galen Clark who served from 1866 to 1879. The second was the same Hutchings who had brought tourists to the Valley in 1855.

In 1868, conservationist John Muir came to what is now the park. He immediately began to write about the area and to fight for its further preservation. His articles, appearing in *Century* Magazine, brought the beauties of the region even more before the American people. It was largely through his efforts and those of *Century's* publisher, Robert Underwood Johnson, that Congress was finally influenced to act again in Yosemite's behalf.

The area granted to the State of California by Lincoln consisted of the Mariposa Grove of Big Trees and the Valley. In 1890, Congress established Yosemite National Park *around* the state grant so there was, in effect, a state park surrounded by a national park. This situation continued until 1906 when the state re-ceded the original grant back to the Federal Government thus ending a period of dual administration.

The history of Yosemite is a fascinating story. It is well told in Carl Russell's book *100 Years in Yosemite* as well as by the fine exhibits in the Valley museum and in the Pioneer Village at Wawona.

Geology

A newcomer to Yosemite Valley, unless he is a geologist, cannot help but wonder "how come?" What formed the spectacular rounded domes, the waterfalls world famous for their height, and the Valley itself with its level floor and its nearly perpendicular 3,000-foot walls? The geological history of Yosemite is shown clearly by working models in the museum, but something about it is not out of place in this book.

Since it is necessary to start our story somewhere, we will pick a time about 130 million years ago when the country now occupied by the Sierra Nevada was covered with a series of low parallel ridges running in a general northwest-southwest direction. Under these ridges were the granites that we see in Yosemite today.

Over millions of years, water eroded the ridges and exposed the granites and produced a land of low, rolling hills and broad valleys. Drainage was then to the southeast into a slow, sluggish stream which was later to become the Merced River.

At length, a great upheaval occurred which lifted and tilted a piece of the earth's crust so huge that it covered the entire area of what is now the Sierra Nevada. This great section, known as the Sierra Block, tilted so that on

the east there was an abrupt escarpment rising from what is now Owens Valley in which such towns as Bishop, Lone Pine, and Independence are located today. On the west, the great block sloped gradually down to blend into what we now know as the Central Valley of California.

The streams which used to be sluggish, because they were flowing through comparatively level country, were now given new life by the increased slope, and they raced toward the Pacific, cutting deep canyons. The old sluggish ancestor of the Merced River, since its course was in a general westerly direction, was among the streams that took on new life and it rushed seaward carving a canyon 2,000 feet deep. The tributary streams feeding into it from the north and south continued on about the same gradient as before because there was nothing to accelerate their pace. As a result, the Merced literally left them behind. The deeper it cut, the higher the tributary streams were stranded above it. Thus were born the hanging valleys and the waterfalls which you see today.

But the end was not yet, for the climate changed a million or more years ago and ice began accumulating in the high country to a thickness of thousands of feet. In time, glaciers began moving down the slopes, grinding and gouging as they progressed, to give the landscape a still different appearance. The V-shaped and stream-cut valleys were deepened and widened by the ice and became

El Capitan, *standing as a sentinal at the lower end of the Valley, is larger than the Rock of Gibraltar and is said to be the greatest single block of granite in the world*

Storm clouds hover over Tenaya Canyon, sprinkling a light snowfall over peaks of the High Country. The mouth

of the canyon is guarded on the left by Mount Watkins while across the canyon Half Dome looms up into the sky

U-shaped. The terrific pressure rounded off great masses of granite forming domes, and in certain sections the weight polished large areas to mirror smoothness.

At least three times the glaciers advanced and then receded, the last advance leaving a great pile of rock debris in the vicinity of El Capitan. This natural dam formed a lake 5½ miles long, giving the Valley its flat floor, and remained until the pressure of the water from the melting ice broke through, draining the lake and letting the Merced River resume its former course.

The glaciers here, as throughout the whole Sierra, gouged many hollows in their slow journey and these hollows filled with water to give us delight in a thousand sparkling mountain lakes.

There are still glaciers in the Sierra, remnants of the once mighty ice sheets that sculptured the mountains. In Yosemite, Lyell Glacier can be reached by trail from Tuolumne Meadows and is measured carefully each year by the National Park Service to record changes.

A final word about the domes, which are famous throughout the world for their number and variety. While many were caused by glaciers, others were formed by a geological process known as exfoliation or flaking. Thin scales become loosened by weathering and flake off, much as an onion would, to give the rounded effect that is so characteristic.

Natural Features

Yosemite Valley is undoubtedly the park's greatest single feature. It is world-famous, and you probably saw a sketch of it in your geography book in grade school. It is 7 miles in length, a little over a mile in width, with walls whose higher points reach over 3,000 feet above the floor. The Merced River rushes into the Valley at its upper end after a tumultuous journey from its birthplace in the High

RIGHT

Two noted geological features *of Yosemite are Lyell Glacier, above, near Tuolumne Meadows, and Lembert Dome, below, seen here from Tuolumne River Bridge*

Cathedral Spires, *directly across the Valley from famed El Capitan, are among Yosemite's well-known landmarks*

Country, terminating in a 317-foot leap at Vernal Fall and a 594-foot drop at Nevada Fall a mile above. The enthusiasm of the Merced is soon spent, however, and it meanders lazily through the Valley. Toward the lower end, it gains momentum once more as if eager to join the San Joaquin a hundred miles to the west.

Itself a single feature of the park, the Valley is composed of many individual features which give it beauty and fame. Most important of these, of course, are the great waterfalls which rank among the finest in the world. Of these, Ribbon Fall has the greatest single drop —1,612 feet. The most famous is Yosemite Falls which is made up of three parts, the Upper Fall, the cascades, and the Lower Fall. The three parts combined drop 2,425 feet from the rim. The Upper Fall alone is 1,430 feet— over eight times the height of Niagara. And there are others such as Bridalveil, 620 feet, Nevada, 594 feet,

Vernal, 317 feet, and Illilouette, 370 feet. While more water rushes over Nevada and Vernal Falls in the Merced River, Yosemite Falls always seems to dominate because of its height and because in spring its thundering roar can be heard throughout the Valley. If you are near enough, the very ground seems to tremble with the terrific impact of the falling tons of water.

The falls are at their height during May and June, and many visitors who come after that time are disappointed in not seeing them at their best or, in fact, not seeing them at all. A few falls will run throughout the summer if the snow pack in the mountains is unusually heavy, but in dry years there is no evidence of them after mid-August. So, go in the spring if you want to see the waterfalls at their peak.

Another feature not restricted to the Valley, although the largest ones are found there, are the great granite domes. Of these Half Dome is king, dominating the upper end of the Valley as it rises 4,800 feet above the floor and looks down upon its neighbors North Dome and Basket Dome. Near Glacier Point is Sentinel Dome, and in Tuolumne Meadows is the famous Lembert Dome. While not a dome, El Capitan raises its massive head 3,000 feet above the Valley floor and seems to salute the visitor as he takes his first unobstructed look from Valley View. El Capitan is a tremendous monolith, said to be the largest single block of granite in the world and much greater in volume than the Rock of Gibraltar.

Yosemite's High Country easily rivals certain parts of Kings Canyon in grandeur. What is more, it is readily accessible, for you can drive into the heart of it at Tuolumne Meadows and save the long hot climb by foot out of the Valley. The High Country is definitely a feature of this park. No one has really seen Yosemite until he has seen the back country which contains beauty undreamed of by the visitor who ventures no farther than the Valley itself.

Only a few miles up the Merced above Vernal and Nevada Falls is Little Yosemite Valley, a miniature of its great neighbor below. There are great canyons like that of the Tuolumne, and there are acres of glacial-polished granite. There are spectacular domes, high wind-swept passes, rugged peaks, glaciers, and many glistening mountain lakes.

Yosemite's trails are good and well patronized both by backpackers and horseback parties. The most popular is the High Sierra Loop, about 50 miles in length, upon which is located the High Sierra Camps. But there are many others, some long and some short, some level and some steep, which combined give Yosemite a total of some 700 miles of trail.

When you plan your Yosemite vacation, plan sufficient time to get into this land of polished granite, lakes, and domes, for it is among the finest in the Sierra and reached with a minimum of effort.

Flora And Fauna

Although the giant sequoias of Sequoia and Kings Canyon national parks are larger and more extensive, it is probable that no single tree is better known to adults and school children alike than the Wawona (Tunnel) Tree ("the tree you can drive through") which is located in the Mariposa Grove, largest of the three sequoia groves in Yosemite. This grove is a few miles beyond the South Entrance of the park, and the other two, the Tuolumne and Merced groves, are located near Crane Flat on the Big Oak Flat Road. A detailed treatment of giant sequoias is given in the chapter on Sequoia National Park and more on the Mariposa Grove will be found under the "Yosemite Regions" section of this chapter.

The meadows of Yosemite are delightful, especially in spring when the ground is moist and the wildflowers are at their height. The Valley meadows were more extensive in the early days but the years have brought an ever-encroaching forest of lodgepole pine and other trees which have overrun some meadows and shrunken others in size. Nevertheless, there are several large lush meadows on the Valley floor.

In the country above the rim, Tuolumne Meadows are the most extensive and best known. Here flowers bloom in profusion and a network of small streams keeps the meadows moist throughout the summer. As in all the Sierra, one comes most unexpectedly upon small, beautiful meadows, sometimes fully surrounded by forest, which are completely undisturbed and through which one can walk sinking deep in the luxuriant growth.

While the flowers of Yosemite are not too distinctive from those of other regions in the Sierra, they are profuse and varied. More than 1,200 species occur in the park, and a botanist can have a field day since park roads give him an extraordinary range of elevation, from 3,000 feet at Arch Rock Entrance Station to nearly 10,000 feet at the Tioga Pass Entrance. In this range of 7,000 feet, he will find a satisfying variety of flora, even along the road, and a much greater abundance if he leaves his car and does some hiking. Along the river in the Valley, the Pacific dogwood and azalea are especially beautiful in the spring. Also found at this time, particularly in the shelter of the coniferous forests as the snow is receding, is the brilliant red snow plant. All flowers, of course, are protected in a national park, and woe be unto the person who picks a snow plant not only in a park but anywhere in

NATIONAL PARK SERVICE PHOTO

Vernal Fall, *reached by a short hike from Happy Isles, is one of most graceful of the park's numerous waterfalls*

California, for a heavy fine results if he is caught.

In general, Yosemite is heavily forested. On the Valley floor are big incense cedars, often mistaken by the newcomer for sequoias, and there are tall ponderosa or yellow pines as well as lodgepole pines. One of the most frequently encountered trees in the Valley is the live oak with its small evergreen leaves. Higher up, one finds the big Jeffrey pine which looks so much like the ponderosa. Here also grow firs and, still higher, the white-barked pine. One of the finest stands of sugar pine remaining in the world was purchased not too many years ago by the Rockefeller interests and presented to the park to save it from being cut for lumber.

Fire, of course, is an ever-present menace especially in summer. Don't smoke while traveling, and if you see a fire, report it at once to the nearest man in uniform. Emergency telephones are placed at frequent intervals along the park roads. Fire permits, which can be obtained from the ranger stations, are required for fires built at designated camping places along park trails. Fire permits are not required in the automobile campgrounds.

You will probably see more deer and bears in Yosemite than in any other California park. Deer seem to be everywhere—in the meadows and along the roads, and they are alarmingly tame. Alarming because it is next to impossible to convince people that such a gentle-appearing creature *is* dangerous. Deer rise on their hind legs and strike with their sharp front hoofs for no apparent reason, and many people are injured each year because they refuse to heed the warning of the National Park Service to leave the animals alone. Bears, too, are common along the roads and throughout the camps where they delight in upsetting garbage cans to the amusement of the visitors and to the disgust of the sanitation crews. The same warning applies to bears as to deer. Leave them strictly alone, for by *not* doing so you may run afoul not only of the animal but of the rangers. There is, by the way, a park regulation which prohibits the feeding of these animals.

The other animals of the park are really not much different from those found in the rest of the Sierra Nevada. About 60 different species of mammals and 200 kinds of birds make their home in Yosemite and many of them can be seen at the museum in the Valley.

How To Enjoy The Park

Your own likes and dislikes and the entrance through which you enter the park will have a lot to do with how you begin your Yosemite adventure. First of all, you will want to decide whether you are going to headquarter in the Valley and work out from there, or whether you are going to stay in one of the outlying areas and visit the Valley on occasion.

By studying the map, you will see that it is possible to reach all of the outlying areas without entering the Valley proper. Even if you come up the All-Year Highway from Merced, you can turn off south to the Wawona or Glacier Point sections or north to the Tuolumne Meadows section before you even catch a glimpse of the Valley, except for views from the road as you climb to the rim. Plan your trip, therefore, so you know where you want to stay and go there first.

If you are camping and don't like your first selection, you can usually move to another spot; if you are staying at one of the resorts, there is always a chance that the reservations can be changed if you wish to sample another area.

Wherever you plan to headquarter, get in touch with the rangers or naturalists if you want advice on how to see the park. You will find attendants at the museums at Tuolumne Meadows and the Mariposa Grove, the observation station at Glacier Point, and the Pioneer Village at Wawona. You can also get information at the entrance station, if the rangers on duty are not too busy with traffic. It is best to go through the entrance station and park your car so as not to hold up others. Then go back and talk to the rangers—if you can find a moment when they are free. If you have decided to headquarter in the Valley, you can consult the information service at the desk in the Park Headquarters and in the Museum, both at Yosemite Village. When you get into the middle of things in the Valley, don't be surprised at the number of people and the traffic you find, for in summer this is a small city and is probably more active and crowded than any national park you have ever visited.

No matter where you stay, you should, as soon as you get settled and somewhat oriented, visit the main museum in Yosemite Village. By so doing, you will get a much better idea of what the park has to offer and be better equipped to decide how you want to spend your time.

While more will be said in the "How Long Can You Stay" section about how best to spend your time in the park, it may not be out of place to offer a few general suggestions here.

As in all parks, you should take advantage of the free, government interpretive programs. They are well organized in Yosemite and are more diversified than in many parks. In summer there are evening campfire talks on a variety of subjects at many points, daily nature walks, short and long field trips, and lectures at several museums. Get a schedule of these activities and join them.

If you are driving, you can purchase two pamphlets that will help you learn a great deal about the park in a short time. They are self-guiding auto tours, one of the whole park and one of the Valley itself. By watching the mileage on your speedometer, following the text in the pamphlets, and stopping at the road markers keyed to the booklet, you will learn something of interest about

TOP
The Junior Nature School *gives children an opportunity to learn about the park's animals, birds, flowers. Here they study the wildflowers in garden behind the museum*

BOTTOM
A visit to the Yosemite Museum *will give you a better understanding of the park's features. In Geology Room, a ranger naturalist explains Valley's formation to visitors*

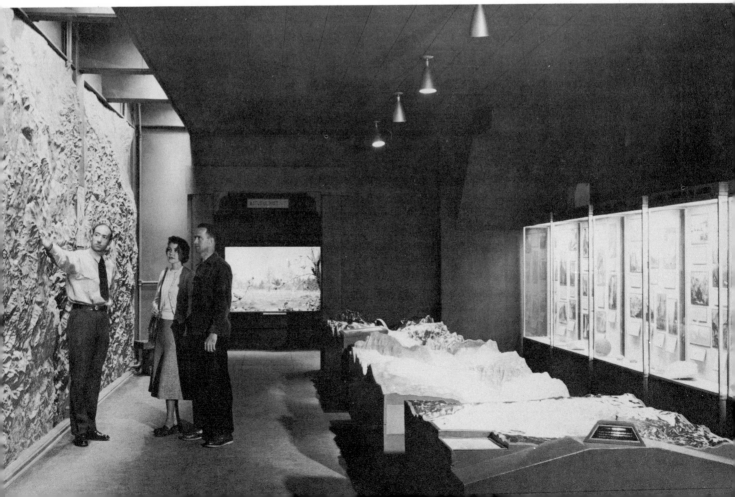

Broad riding trails, *like this one near Happy Isles, are a popular feature of the Valley. You can take guided trips to outlying areas or explore the Valley floor on your own*

Early autumn *is an ideal time for a bicycle tour of the Valley floor. Level roads are free of heavy summer traffic, and the trees are beautiful with brilliant autumn color*

every important feature that can be seen from any road in the park. The pamphlets are inexpensive and well illustrated.

In almost every locality, especially the Valley, there are all types of trails—long, short, steep, and level—that will lead you to fascinating spots along the river or to shady retreats under the high cliffs.

Horseback riding is popular both in the Valley and in the outlying areas. Whether you want to ride for an hour or a day or take a pack trip, it can be arranged. In the Valley, bicycling is popular and the roads are ideal for the purpose.

If you like to swim, there are pools at Camp Curry, Yosemite Lodge, and the Wawona Hotel. Golf or tennis? Both are available at The Ahwahnee and at the Wawona Hotel and you don't have to be a guest to enjoy them.

Dancing is offered every night during the summer season at both Camp Curry and The Ahwahnee and, during the "off season," on certain nights at The Ahwahnee hotel.

All in all, there are few national parks that offer such a variety of things to do as does Yosemite.

Yosemite Regions And What To Do In Each

Perhaps it would be better to give this section some such title as "Yosemite's Centers of Concentration," because it is difficult to partition a park such as this into regions. However, for the sake of clarity and to familiarize you with the various activities in the park, we will discuss general areas, call them what you like.

The Valley

Here in the Valley you will find the administrative offices of the National Park Service, the Yosemite Park and Curry Co., the hospital, the major stores, and shops. About 80 percent of the campground space is located here as is a large percentage of the lodge and hotel accommodations. During the last several years, more than a million people

CLYDE CHILDRESS

Mist Trail *leads from Happy Isles to the top of Vernal Fall. This is a wet hike in spring when spray drenches the trail, but you can dry out in warm sunshine at the top*

The Merced River *is high in early summer when it is fed by the run-off from mountain streams. There are fish in the river, but you'll have more success in the back country*

have come to the park annually, and by far the greater portion of these have stayed in the Valley. It is not surprising, therefore, that most of the activities are centered here, especially since, during the summer, there are peak times when more than 33,000 people are sleeping in the campgrounds and rented accommodations. This "sleeping area," by the way, totals only about one square mile. The Valley, therefore, is a small city in summer with conditions probably not too unlike those found at home. You should remember this before planning your vacation. If this is what you want, you will enjoy yourself immensely; but if it is not, and you *must* vacation between mid-June and the first of September, you should consider one of the outlying sections where conditions may be more to your liking. There is, however, another alternative.

If you can visit the Valley in May or early June, or in September or October, you will find conditions much different and possibly more to your liking. Most of the facilities are operating (many are open the year around),

you will not find the crowds, it is not so hot, and the landscape is at its best. In the fall, the colors are brilliant. As long as there is foliage on the oaks and maples and dogwoods and poplars, there is gold and red against the sky and cliffs. In the oak woods, you can kick along through ankle-deep leaves and brittle brown ferns. The air is clear and sparkling, and if you have visited the Valley in summer, you will be amazed at how quiet it can be in autumn.

Spring has been called Yosemite's season of exuberance. Then the redbud, advance guard of a thousand wildflower varieties, blooms while there is still snow on the ledges of the south wall. Then come the dogwood and the azaleas and the water—the melting snow swells the streams, and the falls pour over the cliffs in thundering torrents. Nothing in the world compares with the spring waterfalls of Yosemite.

Among the various things to do in the Valley, wandering along the many trails is one of the most enjoyable. This isn't *hiking*, it is *strolling*. The trails are wide, usu-

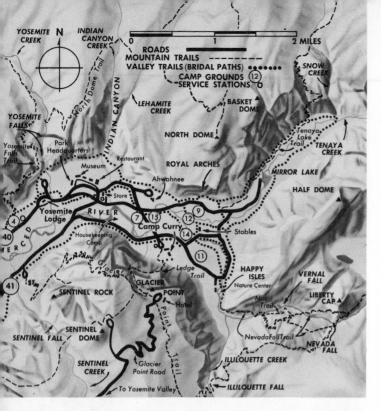

Upper end of Valley, *shown here, has most "civiliza-tion." To west are beaches, Bridalveil Fall, and El Capitan*

ally shady, comparatively level, and lead to all sorts of out-of-the-way places. For example, there is a beautiful quarter-mile trip to the foot of Yosemite Falls where, as you approach the end of the walk, you can feel the spray on your face. If you are looking for something a little more strenuous, you can continue on as far as you wish along the Yosemite Falls Trail. From Happy Isles (and you should do this if at all possible), you can take the trail about 1½ miles in length to the top of Vernal Fall. There you can lie on the smooth granite and watch the water as it drops the 317 feet. If you are not tired, go on for another mile to Nevada Fall, which drops 594 feet. If you are looking for something even more strenuous, climb the wall to Glacier Point over the Four-Mile Trail (it is nearer five), which starts near the base of Sentinel Rock.

If you don't care for walking but like to ride a bicycle, you can rent one at the Lodge or Camp Curry by the hour or day. You will find that bicycling is a favorite sport here. It is a leisurely and easy way to visit various points in the Valley.

Horses can be rented at the Yosemite Stables, and while many people prefer to take all-day trips to the rim, others use the cool shaded bridle paths which wind over the Valley floor.

Few national parks offer such an extensive interpretive program as does Yosemite, especially in the Valley. There are two museums which you should visit, the main museum in Yosemite Village and the smaller Nature Center at Happy Isles. The former is the headquarters for all interpretive activities in the park and contains excellent exhibits on geology, natural and human history. You will enjoy walking over the cool path of the wild-flower garden back of the museum, watching the Indian demonstration, and hearing the talks which are given there daily. The youngsters especially will be delighted with the reptile talk using live specimens.

Then there is the museum at Happy Isles which, although originally planned for the children, is popular with adults as well. The pool of *big* trout is a special feature.

At these museums, you can ask any question from "What kind of bird did I see?" to "Where's the other half of Half Dome?" It is the job of the ranger natural-ists to satisfy the curiosity of the visitors and to interpret the park features for them, and they do both in a master-ful manner.

In addition to the museums, there are all kinds of conducted trips, from short bird walks to all-day hikes. Campfire programs feature a different topic each night, as well as high-fidelity music and community singing. These are offered at several campgrounds, and a natural-ist talk is a regular part of the programs each evening at the Lodge and Camp Curry. The Junior Ranger pro-gram is a nature school with headquarters at the Happy

This diagram shows *how the Valley collects back coun-try's snow-fed streams, which provide the array of falls*

Students of natural history, *like this group from San Jose State College, frequently come to Yosemite to hold* *classes out-of-doors and to take advantage of excellent naturalist program that the Park Service offers to visitors*

Saddle horse party *with guide is enroute to Nevada Fall and Little Yosemite Valley beyond. Stables are at Camp* *Curry and Yosemite Lodge, and you can arrange for guided one-day trips or for extended pack trips into back country*

Isles Nature Center. It meets every weekday morning from 9 to 12 with several campfires also on the schedule. The school is limited to youngsters from 8 to 12 years old. Here they learn about Yosemite's animal life, rocks, trees, and flowers. A badge is given upon completion of the course and the boys and girls are permitted to take home the scrap book they have made as a reminder of their Yosemite visit. There is a nominal fee for this school, sufficient to pay for the materials used. The children have great fun and take it most seriously, but parents should remember that this is not a baby-sitting proposition, so don't enroll your child just so you can swim.

The Sierra Club maintains an excellent conservation exhibit in LeConte Memorial Lodge near Camp Curry. Drop in and get acquainted with these people.

There are other spots to visit. Happy Isles itself is delightful, especially in the early morning and evening. Here the Merced River breaks up into fingers and flows around several tiny islands. It is an interesting place at any time of day, for it is a trail hub and you will see backpackers and horseback parties taking off and returning from the High Country.

You should go some evening or early morning down the main road and take the little side road in front of El Capitan. Stand at the base of this great granite mass and look up and marvel.

Covered bridge at Wawona, *a relic of the past, looked like this before the National Park Service restored and* *strengthened it. Original bridge was built in 1858 and was a simple open structure; it was covered over in 1875*

Spend some time in the little pioneer cemetery across the road from the museum. Here lie Galen Clark and James Hutchings, guardians of Yosemite after Lincoln granted it to California. Here also are many of the old Yosemite Indians. Some are known, others have wooden markers stating simply "Boy," "Lucy," and "Mother of Lucy."

You should visit Mirror Lake at the upper end of the Valley. Impressive Easter Services are held here each Easter morning.

If you are staying at the Lodge or Camp Curry or The Ahwahnee, take your car some evening at dusk and drive through one of the big campgrounds—Camp 14 or Camp 11. Here, with the fragrant smoke of hundreds of fires hanging among the trees, you will see democracy at its best. You will find battered old Fords parked near sleek Chrysler Imperials, and the owner of the Ford, who may be a service station attendant from Grinnell, Iowa, will be swapping fish lies with the driver of the Imperial, who is a bank president from Los Angeles.

The Wawona region

Near the South Entrance of the park, at about the same altitude as the Valley, (that is, 4000 feet), the Wawona region is a favorite area of many who want a comparatively low altitude.

A few of the giants *in the Mariposa Grove of Big Trees. This is the largest of the three groves of giant sequoias in Yosemite and contains over 200 trees that are more than ten feet in diameter. Famous Wawona Tree is located here*

There is one campground. It accommodates 160 camps and is equipped with tables, benches, piped water, flush and pit toilets. It is a long campground and stretches for some distance along the South Fork of the Merced River. There is a store at Wawona, a mile distant.

There are two principle places to stop in this region: the Wawona Hotel and Big Trees Lodge, both of which are described under "Factual Information." No matter where you stay in the Wawona region, you should plan at least one dinner at the hotel, which is informal but where gracious living is the keynote. You should also plan to have lunch on the patio of rustic Big Trees Lodge.

Near the Wawona Hotel is a covered bridge which you should see, for such structures are rapidly disappearing from our country. The original bridge was built as an open structure by Galen Clark in 1858; it was later covered by the Washburn brothers in 1875. But the years took their toll, and it was so weakened by age and periodic high water that it became unsafe and was even in danger of being washed away. The National Park Service, realizing its unique quality and historical significance, has recently reconstructed it, using as many of the original timbers as possible so that it now constitutes an historical exhibit. It has become the nucleus for the Wawona Pioneer Village where, in addition to the bridge, you may be interested to see exhibits which tell the story of early Yosemite life, including methods of mining and transportation in that region. Pioneer Village contains old stage coaches, pieces of mining machinery, as well as authentic cabins and houses that will enable you to visualize Yosemite life in pioneer days.

The Mariposa Grove of giant sequoias is probably the outstanding feature of the Wawona region. When you were a child you probably heard about this grove to the exclusion of any other, even those in Sequoia National Park, for it contains the famous Wawona Tree through which you can drive. The tunnel was cut in 1881 to permit the passage of horse-drawn stagecoaches.

There are over 200 trees in the Mariposa Grove that are ten feet or more in diameter and thousands of smaller ones. The largest tree, and probably the oldest one, in Yosemite is the Grizzly Giant which approaches Sequoia's General Sherman in size, with a height of 209 feet and a basal diameter of 34.7.

When you wander through the groves, keep on the trails, for there is certain evidence that some of the trees are endangered by "human erosion." For nearly a hundred years, millions of visitors have walked under those trees, and each pair of feet wears a little of the soil away, bringing the life-giving roots ever nearer the surface of the ground.

Under the great trees is a rustic log structure that houses exhibits about the sequoias. This cabin is even more interesting than the exhibits which it contains. The original cabin was built in 1885-86 by Galen Clark and was used as a sort of rest stop and a place where "natural curiosities" were sold. By the 1920's the cabin was in a bad state of repair and was rebuilt on the original site, using as much of the old lumber as possible and duplicating the appearance of the original. It is quite possible that before long the cabin will be changed, at least in location, for there is thought of moving it near the South Entrance. Talks are given at the cabin each day by the ranger naturalists.

Be sure to drive as far as you can beyond the museum, which isn't much over 2 miles, where the road terminates at Wawona Point. From here a beautiful panorama unfolds of the country below and beyond.

Newton B. Drury, former Director of the National Park Service, once gave a talk in the Mariposa Grove at a time when all national park superintendents were gathered in conference at Yosemite. He said, "The less one tries to put in words the importance of the sequoias, whether it be the Big Trees of the Sierra or the Coast Redwoods, the more nearly one begins to succeed in recognizing their greatness," and he went on to quote from the California poet, Edwin Markham. "These mighty trees belong to the silences and the millenniums. Many of them have seen a hundred human generations rise, give off their little clamors, and perish. They chide our pettiness. They rebuke our impiety. They seem indeed to be forms of immortality standing here among the transitory shapes of time."

Glacier Point

This spot should be visited even though you may not headquarter there. You will find a large campground about 8 miles from the Point at Bridalveil Creek and a smaller campground nearer the Point. Glacier Point Hotel has been discussed under "Factual Information."

The view is the thing at Glacier Point, whether it be in the daytime or at night. During the day you have a tremendous sweep of the Valley in both directions. Half Dome is at your front door; beyond rise the snow-clad peaks of Yosemite's back country. Below, you look into a world of miniatures, for from 3,214 feet above, cars look like toys and people like ants. The Ahwahnee appears as a doll's house and the other buildings in the Valley are correspondingly smaller. The Merced River is a tiny creek, and the roads are a network of dark ribbons.

Darkness brings another world—a world of fireflies, some moving in slow orderly procession and others remaining stationary. Frequently, especially at Firefall time, smaller lights are seen to wink over the Valley floor. These are flashlights turned toward Glacier Point in friendly signaling gestures. And again during the Firefall, frequent bursts of illumination are the flash bulbs as photographers try fruitlessly to capture the scene on film.

While the view *is* the thing at Glacier Point, and no one would dispute this, there are other things to enjoy. For example, you will want to visit the Glacier Point Lookout not only to drink in the view but to study the exhibits in this semi-open structure a few hundred yards from the hotel.

You should also get to the top of Sentinel Dome, which is a fine example of the exfoliated domes mentioned in the section on geology. This dome is reached by a spur that leaves the main road less than 2 miles from the hotel. On top there is a mountain finder which points out the principle features that can be seen from there as well as the oft-photographed Jeffrey pine which seems to grow out of the rock itself. You can drive to within about 300 yards of the top, which leaves a climb of 100 feet, or you can walk the whole distance from the hotel in less than an hour. Or go one way by trail and return to the hotel by road.

Speaking of roads, try the beautiful narrow one that winds its way through the forest and around lush meadows between the Badger Pass Ski Area and Bridalveil Creek Campground. This is the old route to Glacier Point which was used for many years before the present road was constructed. There are few people who know about it, or at least who use it today, but it is a charming little road and part of that charm lies in its abandonment.

If you want to hike, you have ample opportunity from Glacier Point. The beautiful Pohono Trail follows along the rim, more or less paralleling it for almost the full length of the Valley, descending at about the Wawona Tunnel, and coming onto the Valley floor in the vicinity of Bridalveil Fall. The entire length of the trail is about 12 miles, but you can go as far as you like.

Another one is the old Glacier Point Trail, now renamed the Panorama Trail, which leaves Glacier Point and drops down into Illilouette Canyon and on, ending eventually at Happy Isles. Then there is the Four-Mile Trail which switchbacks down the canyon wall to the Valley. Many people take the bus to Glacier Point, spend the night there, and hike back over one of these trails. Arrangements can be made for the bus to return your luggage to the Valley.

If you stay overnight, you will, of course, want to watch the men "push the fire over" for the famous Firefall. While this is admittedly a show and something about as artificial as one can imagine in a national park, it has become more or less a tradition in Yosemite and is continued by popular demand.

Each day about half a cord of bark taken from fallen red firs is gathered and transported to Firefall Point. The fire is lighted about two hours before it is to be pushed over, and by the time it is ready, it has burned down to a mass of embers about the size of walnuts. When the vocal signal is called up from Camp Curry, the coals are pushed slowly over the cliff with long iron pushers. There is no danger from fire since the embers come to rest on a wide ledge about a thousand feet below the point. The Firefall is held every evening during the summer, twice weekly (weather permitting) during the winter.

The Firefall probably originated with James McCauley in 1871 or 1872. McCauley was an early settler and built the Four-Mile Trail from the Valley. Where he got the idea, no one seems to know—perhaps from the legend of Indian signal fires from high points. At any rate, after the first few times, McCauley, seeing that the event was popular with Valley visitors, began to capitalize on the idea and began to charge for the show, $1.50 being the standard price which was easily taken up as a collection from the viewers. Now the Firefall is handled by the Yosemite Park and Curry Co., and there is no charge to watch it.

As at all important centers, you will find a ranger naturalist at Glacier Point. An outdoor campfire talk is offered several nights a week as well as short guided trips in the daytime.

Tuolumne Meadows

To a good many people, the choicest section of Yosemite is Tuolumne Meadows. Here you are at the gateway to the High Country—in fact you are *there,* because this, the largest and one of the most beautiful of the sub-Alpine meadows in the entire Sierra, lies at an elevation of 8,600 feet. (One thing that previous visitors should know about, and something which will interest you if it is your first visit, is the vast acreage of forest that has been killed by the lodgepole needle miner. Most of this destruction occurs between Tenaya Lake and Tuolumne Meadows, and the National Park Service, in an attempt to halt the spread of the epidemic, has been spraying the insects from the air during the past few years.) Those who know Tuolumne Meadows usually love the area and return year after year, arriving with a sense of relief at leaving the crowds behind. Those who do not know it soon learn to appreciate the clear sparkling air, the freedom from noise, the feeling of spaciousness, and the atmosphere of informality.

Glacier Point Overlook *is a breath-taking view point. View here is into upper end of the Valley. Vernal Falls is in* *background, and beyond are snowy peaks of Yosemite's High Country. The lookout also offers interesting exhibits*

True, there is not "so much doing" here as in Yosemite Valley. There are no dances, no golf, no tennis, and you will rarely find a bridge game in progress. But the newcomer finds that the things that await him at Tuolumne Meadows and in the vicinity are equally enjoyable, and he may learn to appreciate them even more. Accommodations, in case you are not camping, are not of the Ahwahnee or Yosemite Lodge type. You live in wooden-floored tents and eat family style in a central canvas-covered dining hall. The meals are not fancy, but you'll get all you can eat of good wholesome food.

Since the campground at Tuolumne Meadows is one of the largest camping areas in the park, you will not have the problem of finding space. It is provided with outdoor tables and benches, piped water, and flush toilets. In addition to a general store and a post office, a gas station and a ranger station are near at hand. A camping limit of 14 days has been set for the Tuolumne Meadows campground.

Tuolumne Meadows is about 55 miles from Yosemite Valley, and it will take you around 1½ hours to get there.

It is 40 miles from Crane Flat Entrance Station or, if you enter from the east over Tioga Pass, it is 21 miles from Leevining. Tioga Pass (closed in winter) is 9,941 feet in elevation, and some visitors who are used to level country are "jittery" on their first trip over. It is, however, "a breeze" for anyone who is familiar with mountain driving. There is really no danger, for the road is amply wide for two cars throughout its length and is well surfaced, so if it is your first trip, don't believe all you may hear about its hazards.

The forty-odd miles from Crane Flat to Tioga Pass is a fine road with wide sweeping curves and scenic vistas. You will find about forty interpretive signs installed at roadside pullouts and overlooks. Part of this road is new, having been dedicated in 1961. This portion replaces a notorious section which was formerly an early-day mining road. It was narrow and winding and meandered around obstacles instead of going over or through them. Progress on the old road was slow, because it was frequently necessary to stop at a turnout to let an oncoming car pass.

YOSEMITE 31

But it was an interesting old road since it offered a comparison between modern speed and the slower days when heavily laden wagons traversed it going to and from the mines.

The National Park Service has retained two sections of the old road for historic reasons. One stretch is about 4 miles and the other about 2 miles in length. It should be understood that these are side roads and not thoroughfares. They are described in the handy booklet *Self-guiding Auto Tour of Yosemite National Park,* which may be purchased in the Village.

There are innumerable trips to be taken from Tuolumne Meadows, and it is the center of activity in the High Country. One of the reasons for its popularity is that you can save a lot of climbing and a lot of time by driving to Tuolumne Meadows and starting any trips you plan to take from there. This way your car does most of the work of getting you to the higher elevations.

Tuolumne Meadows is the main stop on the trail loop of 50 miles that is commonly referred to as the High Sierra Loop. There are six camps on the loop; and if you leave from the Valley, they are, in order, Merced Lake Camp (7,100 feet), Vogelsang Camp (10,000 feet), Tuolumne Meadows Camp (8,600 feet), Sunrise (9,400), Glen Aulin Camp (7,800 feet), and May Lake Camp (9,270 feet). The camps are spaced about a day's hike (about 10 miles) apart and provide good food, lodging, and showers. See "Factual Information" for rates. These camps are a boon for the hiker who doesn't want to carry a 40-pound pack of food and equipment— you need to carry only your personal effects.

Each Monday from late June to September, a Ranger-Naturalist guide starts out with a group on the Seven Day High Sierra Hiking Trip. Their itinerary includes one night each at Glen Aulin Camp, May Lake Camp, and Sunrise Camp; two nights at Merced Lake Camp; then one night at Vogelsang Camp; and return to Tuolumne Meadows on the seventh day. The rate of $25 includes the guide service and the lodgings which are dormitory-type tents. Meals are extra: breakfast and lunch are $1.50, dinner is $3. Groups are limited to 15 persons. Children from 12 to 18 are accepted when accompanied by an adult, but there is no reduced rate for children. A $10 deposit is required for each person. Make reservations early.

It is not necessary to go with a party, although you will miss a lot of fun and good fellowship by not doing so. You can go by yourself, stopping over as long as you wish at each camp to rest, fish, or explore the country. You should make advance reservations with the company even if you don't plan to go with the regular group.

Three times weekly during the summer, the company offers six-day saddle trips led by experienced guides. Trips are limited to ten persons, and total cost is $96. Reservations and a $25 deposit are required. Four-day saddle trips depart from Tuolumne Meadows and stop overnight at Glen Aulin Camp, May Lake Camp, and Sunrise Camp. Total cost is $60; deposit $15. For further details, write to Yosemite Park Company.

Now back to Tuolumne Meadows. If you want to see another camp yet don't want to do much hiking, drive your car a mile or so beyond Tenaya Lake to May Lake Junction on the right-hand side of the road. It is an easy hike of a mile (uphill) to the camp. The lake lies at an elevation of 9,270 feet at the base of Mount Hoffman. Stay overnight, or have lunch there and return in the afternoon.

A slightly longer, but memorable, trip is down the Tuolumne River to Glen Aulin Camp. It is about 7½ miles from the store—you can drive 1½ miles of it and leave your car—and it's downhill all the way. Stop over for a day and walk 3 miles farther to the famous Waterwheel Falls of the Tuolumne which, of course, are best in spring. On the return trip from Glen Aulin, it is necessary to climb only about 800 feet.

If you are looking for a trip that is longer and a little harder, take the trail to Vogelsang Camp—about 7 miles away, with a rise of 1,500 feet. This camp is just about at timberline in the heart of some magnificent scenery. Stay over a day and get some good fishing and then come back to Tuolumne on the third day.

There are many other interesting spots out of Tuolumne Meadows, some reached by short hikes and some by longer ones, and the naturalist or one of the rangers will be glad to discuss the possibilities with you.

This place offers probably the best accessible fishing in the park. If you are lucky enough to get a campsite on the river, and if you are skillful, you can catch fish right in front of your tent. There are many good fishing lakes and streams easily accessible from the Meadows and from the Tioga Road.

The ranger naturalists hold campfire programs several nights each week at the campfire circle in the campground,

TOP
Siesta Lake, *peaceful as its name, is located on the Tioga Road near White Wolf. Its clear, placid waters offer good wading, and you can enjoy a picnic on its sunny shores*

BOTTOM
Merced Lake Camp *is typical of High Camps maintained by Yosemite Park and Curry Co. You can visit camps on guided hiking or saddle trips, or you can go on your own*

Short climbs *above floor of the Valley will reward you with sweeping views in all directions. The photography* *enthusiast will find endless possibilities for picture taking along the more than 700 miles of trails in the park*

and daily nature walks and hikes afield are conducted here as at the other spots in the park. The children's nature walks are very popular. Visitors are always welcome at the small museum and information office at the edge of the campground near the store.

All in all, Tuolumne Meadows is a delightful spot to spend a few days, a week, or a month. If you are looking for a place where there are conveniences but no luxuries, people but no crowds, and plenty of things to do that make a national park vacation worth while, then you need look no farther.

How Long Can You Stay?

No matter how much time you have, you will probably wish you had more for your Yosemite vacation. This is not only because there are so many things to see and do, but because the park has a haunting appeal that intensifies as departure time approaches. This is the reason it has been necessary to limit the stay in public campgrounds.

If you can stay as long as you wish, there is no need for you to read this section, for in time you will probably do all the things that are suggested here. But if your time is limited, perhaps some of these ideas of what to do will make your trip more beneficial.

Things to do in two days

Plan to spend the first day in the Valley and to visit the museum the very first thing. A couple of hours at the museum will give you a good background for what you are going to see in your two days. After that, take a tour of the Valley floor, either in your own car or on a rented bicycle. Tours by bus are also available, but if you take one, you may want to readjust the time of your museum visit. Some of the "must" stops in the Valley are Happy Isles and its Nature Center (the children will love it), Mirror Lake, Valley View, and El Capitan. You can get a better idea of the size of the latter by taking a narrow little road which leaves the main road and swings in close to the base. There is one short walk of a quarter mile which you should take. Drive your car to the Yosemite

Tenaya Lake, *one of the most beautiful lakes in the High Country, is a favorite camping spot. It is situated on the* *Tioga Road near Tuolumne Meadows and is one of the few High Country lakes that can be reached by automobile*

Falls Parking Area and walk at least as far as the rustic bridge over Yosemite Creek. Some say the bridge is enchanted and that if you listen you will hear voices in the stream. Enchanted or not, from this point you will get a much better idea of the terrific power and volume of Yosemite Falls.

Before dinner, go to the El Dorado Diggin's in The Ahwahnee for a cocktail. If you don't drink, go anyway to see the interior of this famous hotel.

After dinner take in one of the naturalist talks. These are offered in summer at Yosemite Lodge, Camp Curry, and at Camps 7 and 14. Talks in the campgrounds are preceded by a half hour of appropriate music. Entertainment programs are also offered at Camp Curry and the Lodge. If you can stay awake after such a day, you can dance at The Ahwahnee and Camp Curry.

On the second day go to Glacier Point. Visit the Overlook there and walk to the rim where the Firefall is pushed over each summer evening. Then go on to Mariposa Grove, stopping en route at Wawona to see the hotel, the covered bridge, and the other historical exhibits. This will put you at Big Trees Lodge in time for a late lunch. Spend a couple of hours among the sequoias, and be sure to stop at the little log museum in the grove (this may later be moved to the South Entrance). Keep on to the end of the road at Wawona Point and enjoy the view from there. You will see "the tree you drive through" on this trip. On your return to the Valley, stop at the parking area at the lower end of the Wawona Tunnel. From here you get an entirely different view of the Valley, and you will find some exhibits that will point out the various features. You might also stop at the Bridalveil Fall parking area farther down and walk a few hundred yards up to the foot of the fall. In these two days you will not have really seen Yosemite, but you will have seen enough to give you an idea of what the park has to offer.

Things to do in a week

Spend your first *two* days in the Valley, doing what was suggested for the *first* day above except in a more leisurely fashion. This will give you ample time for a short hike from Happy Isles to the top of Vernal Fall—a hike of only 1½ miles but mostly up. If you go in the spring, be prepared for a drenching from the spray (and keep your camera covered), for at that time of year, when all the falls are at their best, the Mist Trail to the top of Vernal is *wet*.

On the third day, get a late start and drive to Glacier Point in time for lunch. Plan to spend the night there, having, of course, made reservations beforehand. It is an experience to see the sunset colors from the rim, to watch the Valley fill with darkness, and to see the Firefall being pushed over.

On the fourth day, go to Wawona Hotel or to Big Trees Lodge (again, make reservations), and spend the night at one of the two. You can reach either of them in time to have lunch there and to spend the afternoon under the sequoias. If you aren't ambitious and don't care about hiking, spend the next day in that vicinity resting up, but be sure after that to drive to Tuolumne Meadows and spend at least one night.

If you *do* feel like taking a moderate hike, leave early on the fifth day and go to Tuolumne Meadows. Spend the night there. The following day, check out of Tuolumne and walk to Glen Aulin Camp (6 miles). If you leave early, you will arrive in time for lunch, giving you the afternoon to hike another 3 miles down the trail to the famous Waterwheel Falls of the Tuolumne. On the morning of the seventh day, you will be sorry to leave, but if you *must* go back, hit the up-trail to Tuolumne Meadows and your car. By so doing you can easily get out of the park by late afternoon.

It is realized that this schedule is not feasible if you don't feel you can afford to stop at the various hotels and camps. However it *can* be followed if you are camping and have a simple set-up that permits you to make one-night camps, because there are good campgrounds at Wawona and Tuolumne Meadows and near Glacier Point. If you go to Glen Aulin, you have to carry in your food and sleeping bag, because it is reached only by trail. There is a trail camp there and also some tent cabins, for which you must make advance reservations through the Yosemite Park and Curry Co.

Yosemite In Winter

Every season is a contrast in Yosemite, and winter is no exception. The Valley's popularity as a winter resort is growing each year—and no wonder. It offers good skiing, snowshoeing and skating, most of the facilities are operating, it is easily accessible, and the climate is ideal.

The snowfall is greatest during January, February, and March, and while January is the coldest month, temperatures are not extreme. In the Valley at mid-day, the mercury will stand around 45 degrees or higher, while at night it will drop to 25 degrees or lower. The weather is cold enough to require anti-freeze in your car but not cold enough to keep you indoors. The Valley usually gets about 90 inches of snowfall throughout the winter months, with long periods of clear, bright weather between storms. Here there are two extremes of winter climate. The north side of the Valley receives full benefit of the sun, and the cliffs reflect and radiate this warmth so that the snow melts quickly and the weather is relatively balmy. The shady south side, however, is usually covered with snow from December to March.

Naturally, at higher altitudes the temperatures go lower and the snow piles deeper. The ski area at Badger Pass, at an elevation of 7,300 feet, enjoys ideal conditions for winter sports.

The Arch Rock Entrance on the all-year highway (State 140) from Merced and the South Entrance (State 41) remain open the year around. The Park Service keeps the roads free of snow in the Valley as well as to the South Entrance and Badger Pass. Although they may not be needed on your winter visit, bring chains with you, for you are liable to awaken some morning to a fall of fresh snow six or eight inches deep.

Yosemite Lodge remains open during the winter months with all the services available in summer. The Ahwahnee hotel is also open, except for a short period in December when it is closed for renovations. One cannot think of The Ahwahnee in winter without picturing its annual Christmas-time feature, the Bracebridge Dinner. Here in the great dining room are re-enacted the festivities at Bracebridge Manor as told in Washington Irving's *Sketch Book*. All the characters of the book are present in costume and all the wondrous dishes described

---

TOP LEFT
Winter scene *at Badger Pass ski area. The snow measurement rod held by man in foreground is 14 feet long, so you can get some idea of the depth of the snow along road*

TOP RIGHT
Chinquapin Ranger Station *is on road to Wawona and Badger Pass ski area. This is one of the roads that the National Park Service keeps open throughout the winter*

BOTTOM
Skiers take time out *for lunch and relaxation on sunny porch of ski lodge at Badger Pass. Lodge offers meals and an equipment rental service, but no overnight lodging*

A lone deer *stands out against the whiteness of a fresh snowfall. Most of the Yosemite Valley deer remain in the* *Valley during the winter instead of leaving for the winter feeding grounds as do those from wilder sections of park*

by Irving—the baron of beef, the peacock pie, the boar's head, the wassail, and pudding are presented formally to the Squire. This ceremony has become extremely popular in recent years, and if you ever hope to attend, be sure to make your reservations at least 12 months in advance. Even though you do not plan to attend the Bracebridge Dinner, if you hope to find a place to stay in Yosemite during the Christmas holidays, either at The Ahwahnee or the Lodge, *make reservations early.*

For those hardy souls who like winter camping, Camp 4, in the warmest part of the Valley, is kept open except during brief periods when the snow is too deep to make camping possible. House trailers may also use Camp 4. Fully equipped housekeeping cabins are available at all times. The general store and many other facilities are open during the winter to serve the permanent population of a thousand employees of the National Park Service and the Curry Co.

The main ski area at Badger Pass is 20 miles from the Valley on Glacier Point Road. Since there are no overnight facilities, you may either "commute" from the Valley by car or bus, or find lodging at Wawona which is not quite as far. Wawona offers a cafeteria in the Ski House on the main level and a buffet luncheon in the Snowflake Room above. Both dining areas provide indoor and outdoor dining. A ski shop provides equipment rental service.

Whether you are a beginner or an expert, you'll find skiing to fit your abilities at Badger Pass. For beginners, there is a gentle slope with a T-bar lift. T-bars are also located on three other slopes of varying steepness. If you don't like the downhill type of skiing, there are cross-country trails, marked and maintained by the National Park Service, where you can get away from the more populated slopes. If you really want to get away, you can ski to Glacier Point, about 10 miles distant, or to the

Shaded south side *of Valley floor provides enough snow for a snowman; north side receives more sun, is warmer*

You'll find a new beauty *in Yosemite after a fresh fall of snow, when every tree and shrub is draped in white*

Ostrander Lake Ski Hut, which is about the same distance. You can secure accommodations at Glacier Point by making reservations with the Yosemite Park and Curry Co. At the Ostrander Lake Ski Hut there has, in the past, been a caretaker on duty, and meals and accommodations have been available. It is uncertain whether this service will be continued in the future, so it *may* be necessary to carry your own food and sleeping bag. Check on this before you make the trip. Approval for use of the building must be secured from the National Park Service.

Ski classes under expert instruction are held each day at Badger Pass, and you can enroll for the course of several days at a nominal price. Special classes are offered for children, and there is even a baby sitting service while parents are on the slopes.

Those who prefer ice skating to skiing will find a large rink in the Valley which is open during the coldest weeks. Skates can be rented from the Yosemite Park and

Curry Co. in the Valley. Snowshoeing is popular with some who prefer this sport to skiing. You may bring your own or rent them at Badger Pass.

Of course a good many people who are not interested in *any* winter sport go to Yosemite during the snow season. They go because they enjoy snow (and it's surprising how many California youngsters come who have never seen snow). And they go because the air is crisp and the Valley is beautiful and because the smell of wood smoke on a winter evening brings back memories.

No one will criticize if you wish to favor your lethargy. It is pleasant to relax in front of a big fireplace at The Ahwahnee or the Lodge and to watch a storm through huge wide windows, or to awaken some morning to a new world—a world made fresh and clean by a white blanket which fell while you slept.

Sequoia National Park

Massive sequoias *of the Senate Group reach upward into sky. Wander along trails beneath their branches, and you are certain to be humbled by age and size of these trees*

PHOTO BY JOSEF MUENCH

How to Get There

By Car: The shortest route to Giant Forest from the north is through Fresno. Take State Highway 180 to Big Stump Entrance Station in Kings Canyon National Park. This 52-mile drive is a long steady climb through the foothills and into the mountains but is all high-gear driving and the road is well surfaced and wide. Two miles beyond the entrance you intersect the Generals Highway. If you turn left and drive for 1 mile, you will come to Grant Grove with its lodge, coffee shop, store and campgrounds. If you don't plan to return by this route, by all means take an hour and stop here to see the General Grant and other trees. (See the chapter on Kings Canyon National Park for details.) The right fork of the road takes you to Giant Forest, 29 miles distant. This portion of the road is maintained year around, but may occasionally be closed by snow. If approaching Sequoia from the south, drive 34 miles on State Highway 198 from Visalia to the Ash Mountain Entrance. Then drive 16 miles to Giant Forest via Generals Highway. The grade is somewhat steep, but the road is wide and safe.

By Train, Bus and Air: Concessioner buses meet Southern Pacific trains at Tulare and Santa Fe, Continental, and Greyhound buses at Tulare and Visalia. Santa Fe train passengers get off at Hanford and take Santa Fe buses to Visalia. The above holds for the summer season. If your trip is made between mid-September and late May, "On-Call" transportation is available but reservations must be made ahead of time (and confirmed). Write the Sequoia and Kings Canyon National Parks Company, Sequoia National Park, California. Dates may vary somewhat from year to year, so be sure to learn when the regular summer service terminates.

Airlines serve both Fresno and Visalia.

Where to Stay

You will not find the accommodations at Sequoia as pretentious as in some of the other national parks. There is no Ahwahnee hotel here as in Yosemite and no El Tovar as at Grand Canyon. Nevertheless the facilities are most comfortable, meals are above average (especially in the Lodge Dining Room), and the rustic nature of the cabins is in perfect keeping with the sequoias that tower above them. Make advance reservations for lodging, and send a deposit.

Giant Forest Lodge offers redwood cottages with bath and canvas top cabins (the beds are excellent) on either European or American Plan. Meals are served in the nearby dining hall, and the central lobby contains a lounge and curio store. Rates for two persons in a cabin with a private bath are from $14.00 to $15.00. Accommodations in canvas top cabins are somewhat lower. The Lodge is open for full summer service from approximately May 25 until mid-October. After the latter date, cottages with private baths are open for lodging only until late October and meals can be obtained at the coffee shop a quarter of a mile away in the village.

Camp Kaweah offers European Plan and Completely Furnished Housekeeping accommodations, and is open all year. European Plan service is in new motel-type rooms, in cottages with private bath, and in rustic cabins without private bath. Rates are the same as those at Giant Forest Lodge except new motel-type rooms are slightly higher. Completely Furnished Housekeeping accommodations are in the clean and comfortable rustic cabins and canvas top cabins, both without bath. A central building contains toilet and bath facilities. Rates are reasonable: $8.50 for a cabin with two single beds. Wood for cooking and heating is $1.00 a sack, and a tub or shower is 50 cents. Pinewood Camp offers Completely Furnished Housekeeping service from early June to mid-September. Rates are same as at Camp Kaweah.

Bearpaw Meadow Camp is discussed in some detail under the section "Sequoia Regions and What to Do in Each" (Giant Forest Region).

Free Government Campgrounds are strategically spaced throughout the park. There are ten in all—6 in the Giant Forest area and the rest at lower elevations. The largest is Lodgepole, 4 miles north of Giant Forest, with 340 campsites. Dorst Creek, 8 miles beyond, is next largest, with 234 sites. Campgrounds at the higher elevations are Paradise, Sugar Pine, Sunset Rock, Lodgepole, and Dorst Creek. All of these are at elevations of about 6,400 feet and are open from sometime in May until sometime in September or later depending on snow conditions. Lodgepole generally remains open longer than the rest—until snow is too deep to make camping practical. Water in most of the campgrounds is shut off shortly after the first of September, but you may still camp.

The above campgrounds have fireplaces, tables, piped water, etc., and all but Sugar Pine have flush toilets. Trailers are permitted only in the two larger campgrounds—Lodgepole and Dorst Creek.

Of the lower campgrounds, South Fork in the extreme southern part of the peak (15 miles south of Three Rivers) and Atwell Mill (about 20 miles off Highway 198 on the Mineral King Road) are the only ones not open the year around. South Fork is open from May to mid-October, and Atwell Mill closes a couple of weeks earlier. Both of these campgrounds are small, with only ten or twelve campsites. Atwell Mill has the advantage of a store 2 miles away at Silver City. The other two low elevation campgrounds, Potwisha Trailer Camp 3 miles north of the Ash Mountain Entrance, and Buckeye Flat 3 miles beyond, are open the year around. Both campgrounds are equipped with flush toilets, tables, fireplaces, and running water. Potwisha also has sites for 44 trailers.

Camping in all campgrounds is limited to 14 days per party between June 15 and September 15. Otherwise, the limit is 30 days. Because of heavy traffic, visitors with house trailers should note that on Saturdays, Sundays, and holidays, between June 15 and September 15, trailers 16 feet and over may not traverse the Generals Highway beyond the Potwisha Trailer Camp 3 miles above the Ash Mountain Entrance except before 9 A.M. and after 5 P.M.

Facilities Available

The General Store at Giant Forest Village is well stocked, and staples as well as fresh fruits and vegetables, dairy products and meat are available throughout the summer season from 8 A.M. to 8 P.M. The store is not open during the winter, but a limited stock of staples is available at the coffee shop next door.

Ice can be obtained during store hours in summer at the ice house at the rear of the store.

Meals are obtainable at the Giant Forest Lodge dining room or at the coffee shop and soda fountain in the Village. The Lodge dining room closes about October 14 and the coffee shop is open throughout the year.

Church Services—Christian Science, Catholic, and Protestant—are held each Sunday at Giant Forest.

Service Clubs: There is no service club in the park itself. There is a Lions Club at Three Rivers and most clubs are represented at Visalia.

Rentals (Equipment): During the summer, tents, cots, mattresses, hiking supplies, etc., can be rented at Pinewood Camp. Ski equipment, clothing, etc., can be obtained in winter at Wolverton and ice skates (figure as well as hockey) at Lodgepole.

Horses can be rented at the corrals in the Giant Forest area. Rates are about the same as elsewhere—$2 an hour, $5 for a half day, $8 for a full day.

Gas and Oil are available at Giant Forest Village throughout the year. Minor repairs and tow car service can be handled during the summer season.

Laundry service is available but you should figure on a week. Laundry and dry cleaning can be left at the store.

Baby Sitting can generally be arranged. Inquire at the desk in the Lodge. Frequently some of the college girls will welcome the opportunity.

Mail, Telephone, and Telegraph: Telephone and telegraph facilities are available at Giant Forest Village, the Lodge, and at all permanent camps. There is a post office in the Village during the summer season; address is simply Sequoia National Park, California. After the season, mail can be addressed to you in care of the Sequoia and Kings Canyon National Parks Company at Sequoia National Park and you can ask for it at Camp Kaweah or the coffee shop. You can also have it sent to you in care of General Delivery in Three Rivers, but in this case it will not be delivered to Giant Forest.

Pets: No kennels are available and, if you take pets, they must be kept under physical restraint at all times.

Fishing

There is plenty of good fishing in Sequoia but, as everywhere else, you should not expect to park your car beside a stream and catch your limit without exerting yourself. Short hikes or horseback trips will take you to spots where you will have good sport. A California State fishing license is required and can be purchased at the store in Giant Forest Village. Certain watersheds are closed to fishing at times and notices are generally posted.

JOSEF MUENCH

The big trees *that guard Generals Highway in Sequoia National Park resemble coast redwoods, but their bark is yellow-brown, and the needles and cones are different*

Sequoia gigantea *or "Big Tree"*

SEQUOIA HAS THE HIGHEST MOUNTAIN in the United States (exclusive of Alaska) and the largest trees in the world. Not only that, but it has the distinction of being California's first national park and the second to be established in the system.

The park was established, of course, to protect the many groves of giant sequoias *(Sequoia gigantea),* for here these trees not only reach their maximum size but are found in greater abundance than anywhere else in the world. As an additional attribute, Sequoia has such spectacular mountain scenery that parts of it rival or surpass that found in neighboring Kings Canyon National Park. Sequoia is contiguous with Kings Canyon on the north and contains, at Ash Mountain, the office of the superintendent who administers both areas. The same concessioner, The Sequoia and Kings Canyon National Parks Company operates the lodges, stores, and coffee shops in both parks.

All seasons are delightful at Sequoia, and accommodations are open the year around. Spring is unforgettable, for then the redbud and the dogwood are in bloom and the meadows are brilliant with shooting stars and lupine. In summer, when at last the passes are free from snow and the High Country is open, the park provides a welcome relief from the heat of the San Joaquin Valley. Even Giant Forest, at an altitude of only 6,400 feet, offers cool nights and days that are not too warm. Autumn is a deliciously lazy season when vegetation paints the mountains and roadsides with daring splashes of color and a purple haze hangs over the hills. Winter, of course, is a favorite with many, not only for snow sports, but because the magic of the stately trees seems enhanced with a soft mantle of white.

History

The local Potwisha Indians of the Kaweah River drainage knew the Big Trees long before settlers moved into the San Joaquin Valley near Visalia during the middle of the last century. One of these settlers, Hale Tharp, went beyond Visalia to run cattle near Three Rivers.

Had he not done so, and had be been a different type person, he probably would not have been the first white man to see the trees. But Hale Tharp was apparently a friendly sort, and he was soon on good terms with the Potwishas, especially their chief, Chappo. As a result of their trust and his friendliness, they took him one day in 1858 beyond Moro Rock where he first saw the enormous trees of Giant Forest.

Tharp was so impressed with the area that he later began spending his summers there in a huge hollow log near Crescent Meadow. Here it was that John Muir, one of the strongest advocates of preserving the trees, spent several days as Tharp's guest and later referred to the place in his writings as the "noble den." The log remains today as a small exhibit and is much as it was when Tharp occupied it.

It was Muir who named Giant Forest, but it remained for James Wolverton, a trapper, to discover its largest tree and name it for his Civil War commander, William T. Sherman.

At an early date, public-spirited citizens and conservationists became alarmed at the rapidly expanding lumber activities that were moving nearer and nearer the Big Trees. One of the last straws was the establishment of a sawmill about 9 miles from Giant Forest. This mill was a part of the ill-fated Kaweah Co-operative Commonwealth Colony whose members believed in sharing only up to a point. They drew the line at sharing the Big Trees for their aesthetic as well as their monetary value.

The outcome, however, was in favor of the aesthetic, and on September 25, 1890, President Harrison signed the bill creating Sequoia National Park which removed the last threat to the finest groves of trees in the world.

Geology

In general, the geology of Sequoia is the same as that of Kings Canyon and that of Yosemite, for all are part of the Sierra Nevada. The story of how this great range was formed is treated in some detail in the Yosemite chapter.

The Sierra Nevada itself is a great block of the earth's crust which, over millions of years, was tilted—sharply on the east and more gently on the west—and then sculptured by rains, winds, deep-cutting streams, and finally by great glaciers.

These ice sheets originated high in the mountains and moved slowly downward, grinding, gouging, and changing the topography to leave the land much as you see it today. After the climate changed and the ice receded to

TOP
Mountain peaks *jut upward all around as you look out from Mount Whitney toward vast upper end of Kern River watershed and peaks of the Great Western Divide*

BOTTOM
Manzanita-covered bench *above Kern River is partially forested with ponderosa pine and white fir. Elsewhere in the canyon, the trail frequently follows the river bank*

MARTIN LITTON

its place of origin, the myriad depressions which it had worn in the granite filled with water to give us the countless sparkling lakes of the High Country.

The mountain peaks of Sequoia seem endless once you are among them. And they are high—seventy-five exceed 11,000 feet.

The Big Trees

There is no doubt that the giant sequoias are the largest of all living things, but there has been some doubt cast recently on whether they are the oldest. It *may be* that certain individual specimens of other species which are noted for their longevity show more annual rings than do the larger sequoias. It should be remembered, however, that the annual rings on the largest of the sequoias have never been counted, and when that is accomplished, it is quite probable that their position of venerability will be established once and for all. Regardless of whether they are the oldest, the sequoias do reach a staggering age. The General Sherman Tree in Giant Forest and the General Grant Tree in Kings Canyon, for example, are undoubtedly between 3,000 and 4,000 years old. And do you know how far back that would take us? The Sherman was probably a healthy seedling when Egypt's Old Kingdom was at its height, and it was pretty well along in its youth when Rome was founded, and it was much as you see it today when Columbus discovered the New World.

This species does not grow as tall as the *Sequoia sempervirens* which is found only along the coast, so that its claim to fame, in addition to age, is in its tremendous circumference. The General Sherman measures 101 feet around the base and the General Grant is larger by 6 feet. At the base, the Sherman has a diameter of 36.5 feet, and *120 feet above the ground* the trunk is still 17 feet through! There is a limb 140 feet up on the Sherman that is 6.8 feet in diameter—this limb itself is thicker than most forest trees found in the East.

Historically, too, the sequoias are old. Fossil remains tell us that during the Age of Reptiles they were well distributed over the earth. Of the many related species, it is believed that all have become extinct except for the giant sequoia and the Coast redwood in this hemisphere, and the so-called Dawn redwood, *Metasequoia glyptostroboides,* believed extinct until a specimen was located in China in the 1940's.

RIGHT

The General Sherman Tree *in Giant Forest is a giant among giants, with a 101-foot circumference and a height of 272 feet. It was a sturdy sapling when Rome was founded*

Hamilton Lake, *at foot of Kaweah Gap, is a hike of a few miles from Bearpaw Meadow where there is a tent camp* *operated by Sequoia-Kings Canyon National Parks Company. At lake you'll find good fishing, beautiful scenery*

The Lodge *at Giant Forest Village is set among towering sequoia trees. Sunlight filters through lofty branches to* *create cathedral-like atmosphere. All of park's housing accommodations and most campgrounds are in this area*

It is thought that most redwoods were destroyed during the Ice Age by the glaciers themselves and that the remaining ones exist today only because they were lucky enough to have had ancestors that grew in spots where the ice did not reach.

There are several reasons for the long life of a sequoia. The bark is extremely thick and almost impervious to fire. In addition, the bark contains much tannin which discourages insects. So with these two enemies disposed of, the sequoias are well ahead of other trees in natural protection. Then too, they seem to have remarkable vitality and recuperative powers, so that when a tree is occasionally scorched or even badly burned by a forest fire, the wound heals quickly.

Man, therefore, is the greatest enemy of these giants, and even that threat is disappearing as more and more of the trees come under federal and state protection. There are thirty-two separate groves of sequoias in the park, and while you probably will not see all of them, you will visit the more famous ones if you follow to some degree the suggestions made further on in this chapter.

Wander, then, alone or with an understanding companion, on some of the less frequented trails under the sequoias. By so doing you will become a philosopher. New thoughts will come to you—new concepts of space and time, for one *feels* the age of these trees. Their size and age will humble you no matter how high your station. Yet, at the same time, the experience will give you hope in the realization that these trees have survived over three thousand years of wars and famine, of success and failure. They have seen the Four Horsemen sweep over the earth many times, yet they continue to thrive and grow and propagate. Walk under the sequoias and your own cares and the cares of the modern world will seem but of the moment.

Flowers And Shrubs

No matter whether you enter Sequoia from Fresno or Ash Mountain, you will be impressed by the changing vegetation as you gain altitude. When it is summer at the lower elevations, it is spring at Giant Forest and often winter in

Ranger-conducted group *learns about famous sequoias in Giant Forest area. You can obtain a free map at the mu-* *seum and follow a good 2-mile trail that will take you to some of the more spectacular groves and individual trees*

certain parts of the High Country. Spring, of course, is flower time; but whether you visit the park in spring, summer or fall, you will find something in bloom. Including the trees, there are about 1,200 kinds of plants here, and while a large number of them will be new to you unless you have made a study of mountain flora, you will find many that are familiar.

At the lower elevations, where the heat of summer comes early, you will find the California buckeye, the fremontia, redbud (glorious in spring), and the chamise. These are plants that must flower and seed before the high temperatures affect them. Bush lupine will paint the roadside slopes with clumps of bright blue as will the great masses of ceanothus whose fragrance you can breathe even from your car. Higher up, especially along streams, the Pacific dogwood blooms with its perfect, large, white flowers.

In meadows and other damp spots you will find great beds of shooting stars nodding on their delicate stems, and you will see the bright yellow monkey flower. Hairbells, bluebells, and Indian paint brush are all conspicuous as are corn lilies and cow parsnips.

Remember that flowers are not to be picked in a national park—leave them for others to enjoy.

Animals

An entire book could be written on the animals of this park, for there are many species to be found from the lower elevations around Ash Mountain to the bare peaks of the High Country. The two largest animals that you may encounter are the American black bear and the California mule deer. In the beginning of this book the danger of feeding animals was stressed so we'll sum it up here in a single word—*DON'T!*

You probably will not see as many deer as in Yosemite (although there are more), but there will be enough—especially in the meadows at sunset. Bears, too, are less frequently seen. While they are all black bears, don't think you have found a new species if you find one of a lighter shade—it will be the blond of the species.

At the lower elevations, especially at night, you will doubtless find the raccoon and the beautiful gray fox. Most animals, except deer and bears, and, of course, the chipmunks and ground squirrels, are shy, and you will probably see more of them at night by the lights of your car than you will in the daytime.

Throughout the forested area, are weasels, marten, an occasional fisher, or rare wolverine. Coyotes are sometimes encountered in open meadows where they hunt mice.

Bobcats and mountain lions are seen infrequently. The mountain lion is among the most timid of all the animals, and you can count yourself most fortunate if you catch a glimpse of one.

In the High Country, mountain sheep are present but seldom seen. The marmot or western woodchuck is fairly common; and more often heard than seen is the interesting little pika, a gray animal resembling a baby rabbit, that lives and whistles at you from the rough talus slopes. You may find his hayfield where he has cut grass and spread it out to dry on a flat rock for winter food.

There are about 168 different species of birds in the

park, and if you have spent much time in the mountains, most of them will be old friends. Bluebirds are common, the Western being found at lower elevations and the Mountain near timberline. Throughout the forested areas is the Steller jay with his saucy crest, while his crestless relative, the California jay, is found at lower elevations. The gray dipper or water ouzel sings and bobs on the spray-drenched rocks of fast-flowing streams, and big golden eagles are frequently seen in the High Country.

If you are interested in birds, be sure to take some of the nature walks with the ranger naturalists and attend the evening programs where frequently the entire program is given over to a discussion of them.

How To Enjoy The Park

As always, plan your trip in advance. Write the Superintendent, Sequoia and Kings Canyon National Parks, for free informational literature.

If you are entering from Fresno, you will come first to the Grant Grove section of Kings Canyon National Park after a long but gradual climb of 56 miles. From here, it is about 30 miles to Giant Forest over the good but somewhat winding Generals Highway. You might consult a ranger or ranger naturalist at Grant Grove since you may want to stop at one of the campgrounds or camps before reaching Giant Forest.

If you come from Visalia, you enter the park at Ash Mountain (34 miles), where you will be able to get the answers to any questions that have been bothering you. You may decide to spend a day exploring the country around Ash Mountain, especially the road to Mineral King from which the Atwell Grove is reached. It is 16 miles over the Generals Highway to Giant Forest, and while the road is perfectly safe, it is winding and rather steep in places. Take your time so that you can enjoy the sweeping views as you ascend.

Don't rush through Sequoia. Two days are a minimum, and a week is better. If you plan to do much traveling in the back country, you had better plan on ten days. At all points, you will find conspicuously posted schedules of free government ranger naturalist activities, such as conducted walks and hikes, campfire programs, etc. Take advantage of these and of the small museum at Giant forest; they will give you a better understanding and appreciation of the park.

Sequoia Regions
And What To Do In Each

The southern entrance to the park is through Ash Mountain, which is headquarters for both Sequoia and Kings

Shadows of red firs fall across trail that leads to Heather Lake at 9,300-foot elevation. The trail starts at Wolverton Meadow parking area. Steepest climb is at beginning

Canyon national parks. However, the Giant Forest region, 16 miles north along the Generals Highway, is the center of activity. The points of interest in the two areas are discussed separately here. The third region for exploration is the High Country, a continuation of the High Country found in Kings Canyon National Park.

Ash Mountain

Since Ash Mountain is at an altitude of only 1,500 feet in the southern Sierra foothills, you will find it hot in summer. Nevertheless there are some spots in the vicinity that are well worth exploring. Good motels and eating places are available along the 5 miles from Three Rivers to the park boundary. Year-round government offices are located at Ash Mountain. Go to the office of the Chief Ranger or the Park Naturalist for suggestions of things to do in the vicinity. Here are two possibilities.

Atwell Mill and Grove

Once you arrive, the place is charming, so don't become worried about the road, which turns off State Highway 198 about 3 miles south of the park entrance at Hammond Fire

Campground in Giant Forest *region of park. There are ten campgrounds in Sequoia strategically placed at high and low elevations. Most have ample room so you can pitch your tent without crowding close to neighboring campers*

Station and *winds* for 20 miles into the hills. The road is wide enough and well surfaced, but there are some fairly stiff grades.

Atwell Mill, established in the eighties, converted hundreds of sequoia trees into lumber while it was in operation. Remains of the old mill can be seen today, and the home of the former operator is right beside the road. When the National Park Service acquired the Atwell Mill area, thus enlarging the park, the wife of the former mill operator was given a life tenure to the home, and she still spends her summers here.

Although many stumps attest to the number of trees that were cut in the early days, hundreds of trees are on slopes that were too steep for the logging methods of that time. In all, the trees are found over an area of about 1,500 acres, which includes the more or less separate Redwood Creek Grove. Of special interest is the fact that a sequoia tree is found here at an elevation of 8,800 feet, which is the highest spot at which this species is known to grow.

You will probably want to do some exploring in the vicinity of Silver City, a former mining town which now consists of a collection of summer cottages. This community is situated a couple of miles above Atwell Mill and is outside the park in the Sequoia National Game Refuge.

Mineral King, at the end of the road 3 or 4 miles beyond Silver City, was another old mining community. Now it is important as one of the main jumping off spots for trips into Sequoia's High Country. Pack stations with horses and burros are located here, and there are several good fishing lakes within a radius of 3 miles. You can walk or ride to the lakes, but the trails are steep since Mineral King lies in a sort of basin out of which you must climb to reach them.

There is a small campground and District Ranger Station at Atwell Mill, and if you prefer a place where there aren't too many people, this area will appeal to you. You will like this section especially if it is hot in the Valley, for its trees and its elevation of 6,645 feet keep the temperature at a comfortable level.

Hospital Rock

This interesting old Indian campground is 5 miles up the road toward Giant Forest from the Ash Mountain En-

Round Meadow *is a peaceful little clearing below Giant Forest Lodge. It is surrounded by tall trunks of stately* *sequoia trees. If you visit this lovely spot on a summer evening, you stand a very good chance of seeing some deer*

trance. There are some pictographs here, and you can find mortar holes in the flat rocks where the Indians ground acorns for food. A series of six exhibits in a shelter tell the story of the Indians who once lived here. Legend has it that Hospital Rock was a spot to which the sick were brought for healing ceremonies. Whether this is true or not, there is ample evidence that the place was used extensively by the Indians long before white men came.

The Giant Forest Region

All of the park's housing accommodations, stores, most of the campgrounds, the museum, and the programs are in this general vicinity. Giant Forest is 16 miles from Ash Mountain and 30 miles from Grant Grove in Kings Canyon National Park. There are many things to do in this locality, so once again don't rush through.

Sherman Tree

At Giant Forest you will live under the Big Trees, the largest and most famous of which is the General Sherman.

Elsewhere in this chapter, we mentioned its tremendous size, but to appreciate these dimensions you must see it, walk around it, and let your eyes follow that massive trunk up and up to the full 272 feet of its grandeur.

Adequate parking space is provided near the tree, and there are paths with occasional benches where you can sit and rest and ponder. A ranger naturalist is usually on duty at the tree during the summer to talk with you and answer your questions.

Without a wide-angle lens on your camera it is not easy to photograph the entire tree, because you cannot get far enough away from it without other trees interfering with your view. However, a clearing which has been cut from the parking area provides a fairly unobstructed view of the tree. The light for photographing is best just before noon—say from 10:30 to 12:30.

Other Groves and Trees

Giant Forest is composed of several groves and many trees. In an hour or two you can stroll over a good 2-mile trail and see some of the more famous and spectacular of these. You should visit the Senate and House Groups, the Founder's Grove, and the Cloister Group. Individual trees which you should not miss seeing include the President, the Lee, the Washington, the Pershing, the McKinley, and the Roosevelt Trees. Then too, there is the Chief Sequoyah which commemorates the Cherokee Indian who devised a phonetic alphabet thus enabling members of his people to read and write. The Austrian botanist, Endlicher, is said to have given the name *Sequoia* to the genus in honor of the famous Indian.

In order that you do not miss any of the trees, be sure to obtain a free map of the Giant Forest area at the museum.

Moro Rock

This huge, dome-like granite formation, with an elevation of 6,719 feet, is about 2 miles from Giant Forest over a well-surfaced road. There is a parking area at the base, and a trail with steps and plenty of spots to sit and rest winds its way 300 feet upward to the top. The sweeping views from Moro Rock are tremendous and give you at least an idea of Sequoia's rugged back country, of which you are little aware as you walk over the comparatively level trails at Giant Forest.

To the west are the low ridges of the Sierra foothills with the flat expanse of the San Joaquin Valley beyond them. The steep walls of the canyons of the Kaweah and its tributaries lie to the south and east, climaxed by the magnificent jagged crest of the Great Western Divide. No visitor should miss this view.

Enroute to the Moro Rock parking area, on the left side of the road, is the Auto Log. If you want to take an unusual picture, drive your car onto the log and get below it with your camera. There is plenty of room, and lots of people do it.

Crescent Meadow

John Muir was so impressed by Crescent Meadow that he referred to it as the fairest portion of all the Sierra. It is a lovely crescent-shaped meadow surrounded by a wall of dark and stately forest trees. A tiny stream runs through it, and the youngsters will be delighted with the many small brook trout that can always be seen toward the lower end. (No fishing, though!) The meadow is boggy and flowers bloom throughout the summer, especially during the early part when the ground is covered with shooting stars, yellow monkey flowers, and other moisture-loving plants.

A good trail about a mile in length circles the meadow and affords a delightful stroll. Crescent Meadow itself is reached by an interesting trail from Giant Forest Village—

about a 2½-mile walk. You can return via Moro Rock for a pleasant hike of less than 6 miles.

The road to Crescent Meadow branches left from the Moro Rock road a little less than 2 miles from the Village. It passes *under* a fallen sequoia which has been cut sufficiently to accommodate cars. This is Tunnel Log, but don't confuse it with the tunnel which was cut *through* the living Wawona Tree in the Mariposa Grove at Yosemite.

A short distance beyond the Tunnel Log is the Mather Plaque, placed in this and other national parks as a tribute to Stephen T. Mather, first Director of the National Park Service. Park your car, go to the plaque, and read the following words thoughtfully:

"He laid the foundations of the National Park Service
Defining and establishing the policies
Under which its areas shall be developed and
Conserved unimpaired for future generations.
There will never come an end to
The good he has done."

About one-tenth of a mile beyond the plaque is the Black Chamber, a sequoia which has refused to die even though only a small portion of trunk and foilage remains alive to furnish it nourishment.

Tharps Log

A pleasant half-mile hike from Crescent Meadow Parking Area brings you to Tharps Log. You can go inside the log where the pioneer, Hale Tharp, spent his summers and where John Muir was a guest.

Sunset and Beetle Rocks

Sunset Rock is near Sunset Campground north of Giant Forest Village and, as the name implies, it should be visited at sunset for the best effects. Beetle Rock is similar and is located west of the Village near Camp Kaweah. If at

---

TOP LEFT
Moro Rock *affords sweeping views of Great Western Divide, Sierra foothills, San Joaquin Valley. You can drive to base, then follow a winding trail 300 feet upward to top*

TOP RIGHT
Tunnel Log, *on the road to Crescent Meadow, is a giant sequoia which spans road and which has been cut sufficiently to permit automobiles to pass beneath its trunk*

BOTTOM
From High Sierra Trail *up Wallace Creek, view is down the U-shaped, forested canyon of the Kern River. The top of 12,305-foot Mt. Guyot can be seen at left of photograph*

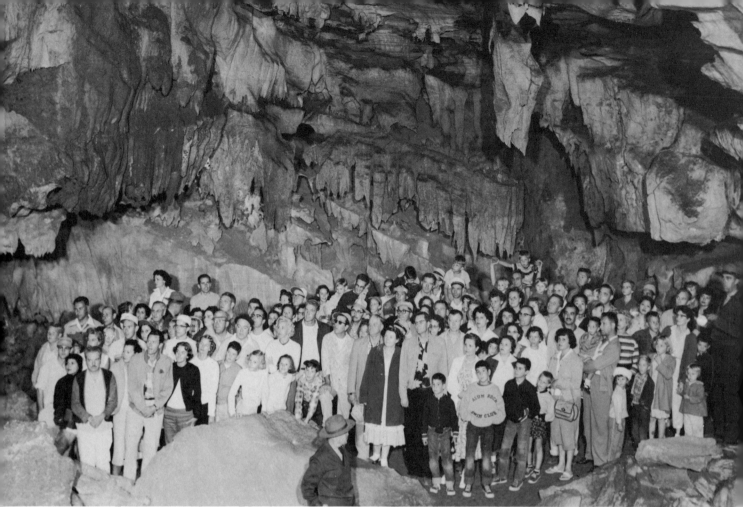

Crystal Cave contains unusual formations which have built up over hundreds of years. Here ranger naturalist explains *the formations in one of the rooms. A half-mile trail leads through the cave. It is cool inside so take along a wrap*

times you forget that there are other worlds besides the human world in which you live, go to Beetle Rock and sit a while and watch the world of insects and birds and lizards and a host of other small animals. And at times when you think life is dull, remember that Sally Carraghar wrote an entire book just about the things she saw in one day on Beetle Rock.

Crystal Cave

The cave is 9 miles by road from Giant Forest, and then a half-mile trail leads you down to the entrance. The trail is wide, well surfaced, and much of it is shady. The grade is a little stiff since the trail drops 320 feet from the parking area, so make the return trip slowly, especially if the day is hot.

There are eleven known caves in the park, but this is the only one open to the public. Strangely enough, this particular cave was not discovered until 1918, 28 years after Sequoia became a national park. Although small compared to some, Crystal Cave contains some beautiful pools

and formations and affords a well-worth-while trip of about a half mile in length. Indirect white light illuminates the cave and shows up the white crystalline marble to best advantage. The trail is good and perfectly safe, and you will enjoy the temperature—a constant 50 degrees. In fact, you may wish to take along a light wrap.

From mid-June through Labor Day the cave is open from 9 A.M. to 3 P.M. Admission is 50 cents; children under 12 are free. It is closed on Mondays and crowded on holidays and weekends, so if at all possible, go on a weekday. The earlier in the day you go, the cooler the return trip to the parking area will be.

As in all caves of this type the formations are delicate and build up very slowly. Don't touch them, for one thoughtless act may ruin a hundred years of nature's work.

Programs

You should find out about the free government programs as soon as possible in order to incorporate them in your activities. Schedules of these are posted in prominent places throughout the park. Talks are given nightly around the campfires in some of the major campgrounds as well as at the outdoor amphitheater across the road from Giant Forest Lodge. An outdoor program is offered at the Lodge, and frequently ranger naturalists participate. In addition daytime walks conducted by a naturalist are scheduled. The museum at Giant Forest (the only one in the park at present) is small, but you can spend a profitable hour there studying the exhibits. A new museum is scheduled for construction in the near future.

Strolls in the Vicinity

The many miles of good foot trails in the Giant Forest area give you an opportunity to take several delightful walks of from one to two hours in length. Mention has already been made of the 2-mile stroll starting at Sherman Tree which will take you to some of the more famous groves and trees and of the trip of special charm around Crescent Meadow and to Tharps Log. Another enjoyable trip begins at the museum and takes you along the edge of Sunset Campground to Sunset Rock. This trip is less than a mile in length and affords some spectacular views.

A walk of about 1½ miles will take you to Huckleberry Meadow with its old squatter's cabin. You can return by a different route or continue on to Crescent Meadow less than half a mile farther.

You can hike from Giant Forest Lodge to Hanging Rock (less than 1½ miles), or if you don't feel particularly ambitious, drive about 1½ miles down the road toward Moro Rock, park your car at Trinity Corner, and walk the .3 mile to Hanging Rock.

For more suggestions on walks in this area, check with the ranger naturalist at the museum.

Alta Peak Trip

If you have a day to spend, like horses and don't care about hiking, yet would like to get away, by all means take the Alta Peak trip. It is 9 miles by trail and will take the better part of the day, but the views back to Giant Forest and ahead to the peaks of Kings Canyon and the Great Western Divide are stupendous. The trip costs $8, and groups are under the leadership of an experienced wrangler-guide. Check at the desk in Giant Forest Lodge for further details.

RIGHT
Pear Lake, *with its setting of high-mountain grandeur, is typical of the rock-rimmed tarns found in granite pockets throughout Sierra. Lake is stocked with Eastern brook trout*

Heather and Emerald Lakes

If you are not particularly fond of horses and still want to get away, hit the trail for Heather Lake (4½ miles) and, if you wish, to Emerald Lake 1½ miles beyond. Heather Lake is at about 9,300 feet, and Emerald Lake is about 500 feet higher. The trail starts at Wolverton, and the steepest part of the climb is at the beginning. If you are feeling particularly ambitious, you can go another mile from Emerald to Pear Lake without much rise in elevation. A winter ski hut at Pear Lake is a favorite destination for cross-country skiers. The Pear Lake trip affords some spectacular views, especially into Tokopah Valley.

Bearpaw Meadow

This is a trip of trips from Giant Forest if you want to get an idea of some of the back country of Sequoia and do not have time to see much of it. Bearpaw is 11 miles by trail from Crescent Meadow—a long but not difficult 11 miles if you hike, but perhaps an easier day's trip on horseback.

At Bearpaw you will find a comfortable tent camp perched on the edge of a tremendous overlook at the base of the Great Western Divide. The camp, operated by the Sequoia and Kings Canyon National Parks Company, offers good meals and comfortable beds. There is nothing fancy about it, but you should enjoy every minute of your stay there. If possible, stop over a day before returning—the scenery is awe-inspiring and the fishing is good.

Rates are most reasonable considering that everything comes in by pack train. Tent accommodations (with two people in a tent) are $3.50 per person. Breakfasts and lunches are $2.00 each, dinner costs $3.00; box lunches can be had for $1.50. Since accommodations are limited,

GEORGE BALLIS

be sure to make advance reservations at Giant Forest Lodge. The camp is generally open from the last week in June to the first of September.

The High Country

With forty-three peaks above 12,000 feet in height and nine more than 14,000 feet, and with the 2,000-foot-deep Kern Canyon (in one spot a wall rises 5,000 feet), Sequoia's High Country is certain to impress even the most scenery-hardened visitor. Add the many glacial lakes and streams and, above all, great Mount Whitney towering to an elevation of 14,495 feet and the total picture is one of unequalled grandeur.

This is trail country. The same conditions of travel prevail as in Kings Canyon. Horses and pack stock are available near most of the entrances, trails are good and well marked. You will find plenty of fishing.

There are many trips to be taken, some longer and more strenuous than others. A few of them are described here, but there are many routes from which you can choose.

From the West

A fine and not too strenuous back-packing trip is from Crescent Meadow to Bearpaw Meadow and on to Atwell Ranger Station 13 miles beyond. The worst climb on the trip is out of Redwood Meadow, but this is less than 2,000 feet and the balance of the trip is downhill. There is a ranger station at Redwood Meadow. You'll see a fine grove of sequoias here and another grove at Atwell Ranger Station. A few miles before you reach the ranger station at Atwell, the trail forks. The left fork goes to Silver City, about a mile up the road from your destination. You can take this route if you wish to avoid the steep switchbacks that lead you to Atwell. If you don't wish to hike back to

LEFT ABOVE
You'll find good fishing in the many streams and lakes of Sequoia's high country. Boy here is fishing for golden trout in tumbling Rock Creek. Sunset Peak in background

LEFT BELOW
Youngster rides *one of pack animals on the trail between Funston Meadow and Coyote Creek in Kern Canyon. Altitude in this section of Kern Canyon is about 6,500 feet*

RIGHT
Kern-Kaweah River *comes from Great Western Divide and makes final plunge to join Kern. This little river is called "the highest, shortest, steepest river in the world"*

PHOTOS BY MARTIN LITTON

Crescent Meadow, make arrangements to have someone bring your car to Atwell Ranger Station or Silver City.

Another beautiful trip in this same locality continues beyond Bearpaw to Hamilton Lake and then up over Kaweah Gap, dropping down into Nine Lakes Basin (a total distance of about 10 miles). The country around Hamilton Lake is beautiful, and once at Kaweah Gap the views are spectacular. There is a climb of about 2,600 feet from the lake to the gap, but when you get there it is an easy mile into the basin, where you will find plenty of camping sites and not too many people. You can spend a day or two or even a week exploring the lakes in the Nine Lakes Basin area.

From the South

An easy four-day round trip of 18 miles for the backpacker is from Mineral King to Rattlesnake Creek. If you want fishing, this is it. Like all trails out of Mineral King, the one over Franklin Pass is steep and made of granite sand. You will climb about 3,500 feet in a little over 5 miles. You can break the climb with an overnight camp on one of the Franklin Lakes, or, easier still, you can get one of the packers at Mineral King to take you to the top. The view from this 11,400-foot pass on the Great Western Divide makes up for the climb.

If you are a lake fisherman, take the trail that goes to the left a couple of miles below the pass. This leads you to Little Forester Lake a mile to the north where you will find plenty of 8 and 9-inch brook trout. If you like to fish streams, Rattlesnake Creek, which the trail follows, is one of the best small trout streams in the Sierra. You can camp almost anywhere in this warm and sunny valley. You'll get some traffic because the trail is used by those going over to Kern Canyon, but not many will pause to fish even though there are plenty of rainbows and rainbow-golden crosses up to 10 and 12 inches.

The Mount Whitney Trip

This climb is not as strenuous as one would suppose considering that this peak is the highest peak in the United States (excluding Alaska). Hundreds of people make the summit trip each year, including many children and "senior citizens."

Whitney can be approached from either the east or the west, depending upon how much time you want to spend. It will take you three days from the east and a minimum of nine or ten from the west.

From the west there are two routes: from Crescent Meadow or from Mineral King. The route from the former to Kaweah Gap is the same as has been described

above. From the gap, the trail drops down into Big Arroyo and then climbs up on Chagoopa Plateau. After crossing the plateau, it descends into Upper Funston Meadow on the Kern River and then follows on an easy grade to Wallace Creek. About 3 miles up Wallace Creek, it turns south to Crabtree Meadow then goes up Whitney Creek to Trail Crest and on to the summit.

If you want to leave from Mineral King, the shortest and easiest route is over Franklin Pass. This route calls for a 3,500-foot climb. It descends to the Kern River via Rattlesnake Creek, then goes up the Kern along the same route taken from Crescent Meadow.

If you have time, the western approaches are by far to be desired because they take you through beautiful and spectacular country of great variety. By going this way, you can see the high country of Sequoia and climb Mount Whitney on the same trip. You can make a circle trip if you wish, returning by one of several routes; or you can go back on the east side, having made arrangements beforehand to be picked up at Whitney Portal.

From the east you can drive to the beginning of the Mount Whitney trail by turning off Highway 6-395 at Lone Pine. Distance to the trail head is 12 miles. This spot is known as Whitney Portal (8,200 feet), and ahead of you is a hike of 13 miles and a climb of 6,000 feet. The trail is new, well graded, and you will have plenty of company. Many of those you see may not be going to the top of the mountain, but are using the pass (Trail Crest, 13,335 feet) to get into the back country of Sequoia.

Horses are available at Whitney Portal, and the round trip to the summit can be made in a day on horseback. The round trip *can* be made in one day on foot from Whitney Portal if you are an able and hardened mountain traveler, but it is much wiser to take two days. Climb to one of the lakes above Whitney Portal and camp there—there are two or three of them stretched out at convenient intervals. By doing this, an early start can be made the next morning and you can get back to camp at a reasonable hour that evening. Even this will give you a day's hike of 20 miles,

TOP
When you stand on summit *of Mount Whitney, you look down on jagged ridge that forms the crest of the Sierra*

BOTTOM LEFT
Turn in the trail *up Mount Whitney provides this view toward the far-distant peaks of the Great Western Divide*

BOTTOM RIGHT
Highest rock on Mount Whitney *bears marker placed there by National Park Service when trail was completed*

NATIONAL PARK SERVICE
U.S. DEPARTMENT OF THE INTERIOR

MOUNT WHITNEY   ELEVATION 14,496.811 FT
JOHN MUIR TRAIL — HIGH SIERRA TRAIL
SEPTEMBER 5, 1930

Heading north *on the Bighorn Plateau, the trail skirts the edge of a small mountain pond and crosses broad, sandy* *flat before descending into Kern Canyon. The knobby bump on horizon at left of photograph is "The Milestone"*

but half of it will be downhill. You will find water along most of the route except the last 4 or 5 miles where there is no water and little vegetation.

How Long Can You Stay?

Again, as is true for any national park, you are urged to take as much time as you can to see Sequoia. You will get more from your trip if you don't try to do two or three or four parks in a two-week period. Do one to your satisfaction and put off the next one until the following year.

However, if you *must* spend less than a week, here are some suggestions for those who can spend a maximum of five or six days in the park.

Things to do in two days

On the first day, visit the museum right after breakfast to get oriented, ask questions, and look over the exhibits. Find out if there is a naturalist-conducted trip through the Congress Group that morning, and if there is one, by all means take it. If no trip is offered, obtain a Congress Trail tour booklet and take the stroll by yourself. It will only take two hours and you will see some of the finest groves and trees in the world. The trip starts from the Sherman Tree (about 2 miles from the museum). This schedule will get you back in time for lunch after which one of two things is suggested. You can drive to Crystal Cave (about 9 miles) if you like caves and if you feel you have seen enough of the Big Trees. Or, consult your map and pick out some other trail under the sequoias where you can wander as slowly as you please and get back when you wish. Figure on a late dinner so you can

spend an hour at Sunset or Beetle Rock. After dinner attend one of the programs either at the outdoor amphitheater across the road from the Lodge, in one of the campgrounds, or at the Lodge itself.

On the second day, pick up a box lunch at the Lodge (order it the night before) or get something at the store. Drive to Moro Rock, see that, and then go on to Crescent Meadow and Tharps Log. A copy of "Moro Rock and Crescent Meadow Self Guiding Auto Tour", which can be purchased for a few cents at the museum or store, will make the trip more interesting. If you can get someone to return your car to Giant Forest for you, go back on foot over any of the good trails—such as the Huckleberry Meadow Trail. If you don't have a car, you can easily make the round trip on foot and not feel too tired at the end of the day. In the evening, either take in one of the programs or have an early dinner and revisit Beetle or Sunset Rock (whichever you didn't see the previous day). If you do this, better take a flashlight, for you may linger longer than you realize and darkness comes on quickly in the forest.

Things to do in four or five days

The above program can well hold for the first two days of your stay. You should, however, see some of the back country before leaving, so on the evening of the second day arrange at the Lodge for horses for the following morning. At the same time, or even earlier, have the clerk make reservations for you at Bearpaw Meadow Camp. Bearpaw is a popular spot so be sure to make your reservations early enough. The next afternoon will find you at Bearpaw—an unforgettable experience. If you can spare the time, stay there the following day and get in some fishing or simply loaf around camp and soak up the view. The fifth day you will return (probably with reluctance) to Giant Forest.

Sequoia In Winter

Whether you are a winter sports enthusiast or whether you simply enjoy sitting before a fire and watching it snow on the other side of the window, you will find that national parks in winter have a great deal to offer. Not all parks, of course, are open in winter, but Sequoia is one park in which you can enjoy the snow either actively or passively.

The Generals Highway is kept open the year around, so you can reach Giant Forest over the same route as in the summer—that is, from Fresno through Grant Grove or from Visalia through Ash Mountain. Of course there are times, as is the case in all mountain country, when an especially severe storm will close the roads for a few hours or even a day or two, but the crews work hard to keep them cleared at all times. You should, of course, carry chains with you whether or not you think you will need them. Before leaving for a winter trip to Sequoia, it is a good idea to check with an automobile club, for they are familiar with the latest conditions. You will not find as many facilities nor as deluxe service in the winter as you will in summer, but there are enough of both to make your stay entirely comfortable.

The Giant Forest Lodge closes about the 26th of October, but Camp Kaweah remains open the year around. Here you will find motel accommodations and rustic cabins that have been conditioned for winter occupancy and are entirely satisfactory. They are equipped with wood-burning stoves (a few have oil heaters), the beds are good, and there are plenty of blankets—if you want more, just ask. Some cabins have housekeeping facilities.

The coffee shop, curio store, and soda fountain, just across the road from Camp Kaweah, are open winter and summer. If you plan to do your own cooking, a limited stock of staple groceries can be had at the coffee shop. The service station remains open.

If your trip is to include winter sports, it is not necessary for you to own or even borrow the equipment. Everything you will need—boots, skis, poles, skates, etc.— can be rented at the park. Nor must you be an expert to enjoy

RIGHT
The Generals Highway *is kept open all year. Whether you go to park for winter sports or just to walk beneath the trees, you will find its snowy beauty breath-taking*

snow sports. At Wolverton, 4 miles from Giant Forest, there are three ski slopes, and you are sure to find one to fit your own abilities. There are two rope tows as well as a warming hut, and the National Park Service has recently constructed a large parking area.

The more experienced skier will find plenty of opportunity for cross-country skiing. The ski hut at Pear Lake, about 7 miles from Wolverton, can be used overnight by making application with the National Park Service.

If you don't ski, but like to skate, the large rink at Lodgepole, 5 miles from Giant Forest, is open from mid-December through February.

But again, you don't have to ski or skate to enjoy Sequoia in winter. If you find the Big Trees beautiful in summer, you will find them even more so in winter when they are draped in their mantle of white. The air is crisp, the stars in the winter sky seem especially large, and a stillness settles over Giant Forest—a stillness in strange contrast to the bustle of summer. So put on your snow clothes and walk along the road some evening after dinner. You will find a new beauty and appreciation in the silence of the sequoias in winter.

MARTIN LITTON

Kings Canyon
National
Park

The John Muir Trail *swings across typical High Country just below Pinchot Pass. It winds along the crest of the Sierra in a lofty wilderness still uncrossed by any road*

PHOTO BY CEDRIC WRIGHT

KINGS CANYON FACTUAL INFORMATION

How to Get There

By Car: The shortest route from the north to Grant Grove is through Fresno over State Highway 180. Distance to Big Stump Entrance is 52 miles. From the south, enter through Visalia either over State Route 65 to Big Stump Entrance or State Route 198 to Ash Mountain Entrance of Sequoia National Park. In the latter case you would, of course see Sequoia first. The Generals Highway connects the two parks and is open the year around. Distance from Visalia to Grant Grove via Ash Mountain is 82 miles. Trail heads on the east side of the park are reached by secondary roads off U. S. Highway 6-395.

By Train, Bus, and Air: Concessioner buses (red) meet Southern Pacific and Santa Fe trains and Greyhound buses at Visalia and Tulare. Santa Fe passengers get off at Hanford and take Santa Fe buses to Visalia. United Air Lines serves Visalia. Concessioner buses transport passengers to Giant Forest in Sequoia, and holders of reservations at Grant Grove Lodge can obtain transportation there on the regular sightseeing tour. Write to Sequoia and Kings Canyon National Parks Company at Sequoia National Park for rates and schedules.

Where to Stay

Grant Grove Lodge is smaller than Giant Forest Lodge in Sequoia, but it is adequate and comfortable. Rates are based on European plan. Meals are available at the nearby coffee shop. Elevation is 6,600 feet.

Meadow Camp in Grant Grove offers completely Furnished Housekeeping Accommodations in rustic cabins and canvas top cabins without bath. Completely furnished, including linens and towels.

Cedar Grove Camp contains a limited number of canvas top cabins on a first-come first-served basis. No reservations are accepted and cabins fill up early. European Plan and Completely Furnished Housekeeping rates are the same as at Giant Forest Lodge and Camp Kaweah in Sequoia National Park. Elevation 4,600 feet.

Free Government Campgrounds are numerous at both Cedar Grove and Grant Grove. They are equipped with running water, sanitary facilities, fireplaces, and tables. Grant Grove contains four free government campgrounds, with a 14-day camping limit on each; trailers are permitted at Azalea campground only. There are also four free government campgrounds at Cedar Grove, with a 14-day limit on each; at Camp 4, there is a designated area for house trailers. Firewood may be collected from specified areas or may be purchased.

Facilities Available

Stores and Coffee Shops are open year-round at Grant Grove and from about June 1 till after Labor Day at Cedar Grove.

Medical Facilities are not available in Kings Canyon or Sequoia.

Church Services, both Catholic and Protestant, are conducted at Cedar Grove and Grant Grove each Sunday from mid-June to the first week in September.

Telephone and Telegraph are available at Cedar Grove and Grant Grove.

Government Interpretive Services: Museums are planned for Cedar Grove and Grant Grove in the near future, but none are available as yet. However, campfire programs and a variety of conducted walks and hikes are offered by the ranger naturalists stationed at both points.

YOU CAN GET A FAIRLY GOOD IDEA of most national parks from the comfortable seat of your automobile: Olympic has its Heart-of-the-Hills Road, Glacier its Logan Pass, Rocky Mountain its Trail Ridge Road, and Yosemite its Tioga Road. Even in Sequoia you can park your car at the foot of Moro Rock and walk to the top for a glimpse of the back country through the panorama of the Great Western Divide. Not so with Kings Canyon, for here it seems that Nature has purposely arranged the topography to guard the rugged breath-taking beauty from the eyes of all save those who are willing to exert themselves to see it. For this is a trail park and unless you take some of the 940 miles of trail either on foot or horseback, you will miss the park's most spectacular sections and you may well wonder why so large an area was preserved.

Study the map on page 47. You will see that Kings Canyon National Park is made up of two separate portions. There is the General Grant Grove section which covers roughly the area formerly known as General Grant National Park; and there is the main section of the park which includes Kings Canyon. These sections are connected by a non-park road 30 miles in length. Both sections are contiguous with Sequoia National Park.

Why have two separate national parks adjoining each other? Why not combine them into a single park? There are several reasons why this has never been done. In the first place, each park is unique in its own way, and to consider Kings Canyon as an addition to Sequoia or vice versa would rob one or the other of an inherent right to greatness. Together the two areas embrace an outstanding portion of the Sierra. Because they are contiguous and their problems of administration similar, both parks have, since 1943, been administered by one man—the superintendent of Sequoia and Kings Canyon National Parks.

The General Grant Grove section of the park is completely dissimilar from the main section in topography

Gas, Oil, etc.: Gas and oil are available at both Cedar Grove and Grant Grove, and limited minor repairs can be made.

Horse Rental: Horses are available at Cedar Grove and Grant Grove. Pack stock is also available at Cedar Grove as well as at many of the trail entrances on the east side. Only packers operating under permit from the National Park Service may conduct parties inside the park. These men are thoroughly reliable and a list of their names and addresses can be obtained from the Superintendent, Sequoia and King Canyon National Parks, Three Rivers, California.

Fishing

It is suicidal to make a flat statement that fishing is good at a particular spot at a given time. The best thing for the fisherman to do is to consult the rangers who are pretty well informed as to local conditions. There are, however, certain general observations that can be made. Here, as elsewhere, fishing is seldom good along highways because there are too many people fishing these spots. Ordinarily the farther you are into the High Country, the better the fishing. Mountain lakes are notoriously unpredictable—a lake may be "hot" one day and completely unproductive the next. A state license, required of all persons 12 years of age or over, can be obtained from the stores in the park. A non-resident 10-day license is available for $5.00. The limit is 10 fish per day per person, but not exceeding 5 pounds. There is no minimum size limit and not more than one day's catch may be in possession.

---

and features. The former is an upland area which gives one the impression of a long plateau, densely forested and with a lush ground cover, especially along the streams. There are no sharply defined topographic features, and the elevation averages around 6,500 feet. The weather is generally cool throughout the summer, and it offers a delightful change as one climbs from the dry heat of the San Joaquin Valley. The main section of the park, on the other hand, is a jumble of massive peaks and deep canyons with rushing streams and countless lakes. It lacks the lush vegetation, except near the streams, and days are warmer at the lower levels, especially on the floor of Kings Canyon at Cedar Grove which is only about 4,600 feet in elevation.

While a part of the present Kings Canyon National Park came under government protection as early as 1890 in the form of General Grant National Park, the rest was not taken over until fifty years later, so that Kings Canyon constitutes one of the oldest yet one of the youngest

NATIONAL PARK SERVICE PHOTO

In Redwood Mountain section *of the park, large and small sequoia trees dot the floor of the canyon. This lovely grove was purchased from private ownership in 1940*

---

national parks in the system.

Kings Canyon National Park was established March 4, 1940, terminating negotiations which began more than two years earlier. There was a difference of opinion on boundaries and, although the park became a reality, compromises deleted some beautiful country such as Tehipite Valley and Cedar Grove.

Flora And Fauna

As would be expected in two adjoining areas, the flora and fauna in Sequoia and Kings Canyon National Parks are almost identical. Only a scientist dealing in subspecies

This woodland *on the floor of Kings Canyon is covered with a thick carpet of pine needles. Large brown cones of* *ponderosa pine are scattered beneath the trees. You'll find the crowds gone in fall, an ideal time to visit the park*

would find any exceptions, and these would be few. Since the plants and animals of Sequoia have been discussed earlier, there is no reason to deal with them here.

Kings Canyon Regions And What To Do In Each

Kings Canyon differs from many other national parks in that no road traverses it; it is necessary to go far to the south or north to get from one side to the other by car. This means, of course, that you should do some planning before you start your trip so that you will know where your activities will be centered. Otherwise, you are liable to find yourself at some east side approach only to discover that you really wanted to be at Cedar Grove on the west side.

To make it easier for you to visualize the park and to plan your trip, we will consider it in two parts: the west side containing the Grant Grove and Kings Canyon sections; and the High Country. The west side contains the

only two developed areas in the park, and as we have said earlier in this chapter, it is reached by car or bus from Fresno or Visalia. The great interior of the park, the High Country, can be reached from Cedar Grove on the west and from the Owens Valley on the east side, where trails take off from the ends of secondary roads that lead west from U.S. 6-395.

If your vacation is to be in the High Country, study a topographic map of the area before you decide on your approach route. You will note that the trails from the east are short and steep. Trail mileages are greater from the west, but the ascent is much more gradual.

Now let's look more closely at the two divisions of the park—the west side, and the High Country.

The West Side

The General Grant Grove Region

The principal claim to fame of this area lies in three Sequoia groves: the Grant, the North, and the Redwood Mountain. The Grant and North groves are within the confines of the original General Grant National Park. The Redwood Mountain Grove is located in the 2500 acres which were purchased from private ownership in 1940 and added, for administrative convenience, to the General Grant Grove section of the new Kings Canyon National Park.

The General Grant Tree, from which the area derives its name, is the largest tree in the park and gives the General Sherman Tree in Sequoia some stiff competition, not only for size but as a favorite among visitors. There are many who prefer the Grant to the Sherman. It can boast a height of 267 feet, only five feet shorter than the Sherman, and it is six feet larger at the base. In addition, the General Grant Tree has the distinction of being the Nation's Christmas Tree, and each Yule Season an impressive ceremony is held there.

Near the Grant Tree and in the same grove stand many other giants of the species including the California Tree whose 260 feet dwarf most of its neighbors. The Hart Tree in the Redwood Mountain section is ten feet higher than the Grant and over five feet higher than the Sherman but it has a comparatively small perimeter—only 73 feet! Near the Grant is the Centennial Stump from which was cut the great tree that was sent to the Philadelphia World's Fair in 1875, before the park was established, and reassembled for the amazement of easterners.

One grove which has not been mentioned and which you should see is the Big Stump Grove, a short and easy walk from the entrance station. See it not for what is there now, but for what you might have seen had it not been lumbered at an early date. Here is an indelible lesson in conservation which illustrates clearly how man can destroy in a few hours something that Nature took over three thousand years to build.

But enough about the Big Trees, for their charm is but one of the attractions here. A wonderful labyrinth of trails radiates from Grant Grove Village. Within an area of 5 square miles, there are over 20 miles of trails, most of which are comparatively level. Some, like the Park Ridge Trail, are especially scenic, while others wind through the groves and along azalea-bordered streams. You will find the trails near the roads well patronized, but a short distance from the sound of cars you can wander leisurely under the giants.

The Grant Grove region is a delightful area in which just to walk. The trails are good and are laid out so that you can usually go by one route and return by a different one. There is practically no danger of getting lost for the area is too small, so strike out and wander and wonder.

While here, you may wish to visit Panoramic Point. Take the road that turns right less than half a mile beyond

MARTIN LITTON

The tumbling South Fork *of Kings River flows through beautiful glacial canyon. The river is high in spring when snows are melting and streams pour down from mountains*

the village and drive to the parking area near the point. From here, you can walk about a quarter of a mile up the trail to the scenic overlook where you will get a sweeping view across the deep canyons of the Kings River to the high peaks beyond.

Conducted trips are also offered in the General Grant Grove region, and campfire programs are held in its new amphitheater.

If you do much prowling in the Grant Grove area, sooner or later you will stumble onto Wilsonia, a 100-acre tract of private land occupied by summer homesites. Here you will find a store, a coffee shop, and an assortment of structures from fine homes to shacks. This area has never been acquired by the government, and you will find conditions different from those in the surrounding park.

The Kings Canyon and Cedar Grove Region

A 30-mile non-park road leads from Grant Grove to Kings Canyon and Cedar Grove. There is nothing spectacular about the first few miles of level forested country, but the thrill of the descent begins as the highway drops 2,000 feet before reaching its destination. By a series of wide sweeping curves, the road drops on a seven per cent grade to the South Fork of the Kings River. The views from these curves are breath-taking, so be sure to pause long enough at the parking overlooks to enjoy them. If the weather is clear, which it generally is, you can look into the canyons of the Middle and South forks of the Kings River and beyond to the bewildering maze of jagged peaks which constitute the greater portion of Kings Canyon National Park. These views are the best hints you will get of the "country beyond," for soon the road drops too low for the peaks to be visible. Beyond and below is the junction where the two forks unite to form the mighty Kings River. With glasses you can make out the surging, billowing water and sense the tremendous power of these streams.

Where the road crosses the river 10 miles from Cedar Grove, you will see the parking area and buildings at Boyden Cave. If you like caves and have a little time, stop and go through. The entire trip, including the ten-minute walk from the parking area, takes only an hour. Trips start at 11 A.M. daily, with the last trip of the day at 4 P.M. The trail inside the cave is about 1,200 feet in length and is well lighted and equipped with hand rails. Most of the time you will be from 450 to 600 feet underground. A guide accompanies each trip and explains the features of the cave. Admission charge is 40 cents for adults and 20 cents for children under 12.

For the last 10 miles to Cedar Grove, the road follows the South Fork—a Jekyll-Hyde sort of stream which at high water becomes a roaring torrent full of trees and brush and with a frightening power that has, in the past, demolished the road over which you are traveling. During mid and late summer, when the waters are low, the river still rushes, but with a musical sound, and a good fisherman can find plenty of sport in the pools and rapids.

LEFT ABOVE

Outdoor exhibits *near store at Cedar Grove are always a popular attraction. If you spend some time studying the displays, you will better understand the park's features*

LEFT BELOW

Grizzly Falls, *located just outside park boundary below Cedar Grove, tumbles over rocky mountainside and pours out its perpetual welcome to visitors approaching the park*

Zumwalt Meadows in Kings Canyon is but a short walk of approximately one-half mile from the nearby parking area. Kings Canyon is a hikers' park, and many good trails lead into back country that is not penetrated by any road

The developments at Cedar Grove—the ranger station, campgrounds, store, and the soon-to-be-built lodge—are on United States Forest Service land which is under the administration of the National Park Service. It is anticipated that within a short time this small section will be made a part of Kings Canyon National Park.

The Cedar Grove area is increasing in popularity, but there is still ample space in the fine campgrounds along the river. Facilities have been located according to a master plan, but the present store, coffee shop, and ranger station are to be replaced within a few years. A variety of conducted trips led by ranger naturalists are offered at Cedar Grove, as well as nightly illustrated campfire programs.

Summer days are warm, for the elevation is only 4,600 feet and the granite walls of the narrow canyon absorb and throw back the heat. Yet, camping is delightful under the big pines on the bank of the boisterous river.

Hiking is somewhat limited in the vicinity of Cedar Grove because of the steep walls which rise on either side of the river, but you can roam up and down the river to your heart's content. From the beginning of the develop-

ment at Cedar Grove to Roads End at Copper Creek is a little over five miles, and the entire distance can be traversed on foot without too much exertion.

If you want an easy walk of about 3 miles, leave the car at Roaring River Falls Parking Area (about 3 miles beyond the store) and take the trail up to Zumwalt Meadows. Just below the meadows, a foot bridge crosses the river thus enabling you to return to your car along the road. If you feel energetic or are getting in shape for a high country trip, keep on past Zumwalt Meadows to the Bubbs Creek Bridge (about 4½ miles), across the creek, and come back down on the other side. Another good trip of about 5 miles each way is from the parking area at Copper Creek up the river to Mist Falls and return. The trail is comparatively level except for the last half mile, and even that is not too bad.

The road ends at Copper Creek where you will find ample parking space. There is a long-term parking area where you can leave your car for a week or a month while you are in the back country. If you have half a day with nothing to do, go up to the end of the road and watch the parade heading into the mountains. It is a picturesque procession—backpackers, long strings of pack animals, horseback riders, and men, women, and children leading burros all pass this way from Cedar Grove as they start into the back country.

The National Park Service has definitely committed itself never to extend the road beyond Copper Creek, its present terminus; so this is literally "the end of civilization." Beyond is the wilderness of Kings Canyon National Park; beyond is the finest the High Sierra has to offer; beyond is High Adventure.

The High Country

Before this breathtaking High Country became a national park, the noted author, Emerson Hough, wrote, "I have seen all the passes and parks in this country and clear up to the Arctic Ocean, and in Europe. There is no country on the face of the earth that compares with the country in this proposed park."

It is not easy to describe the High Country, for such a description must encompass the five senses. It is not enough to describe what one sees—the peaks, gray at midday, pink with early morning and evening glow, and silhouetted against a star-studded sky at night; the unending miles of granite above timberline, with a hundred lakes glistening in glacial-carved depressions; the high passes, snow-choked until midsummer and defying access to all but the birds and the winds; the birthplace of streams in high boggy meadows ablaze with bloom; and the streams themselves, noisy in their impatience to join the main river. Nor is it enough to describe the sounds—the chattering of a pine squirrel or the whistling of a marmot; the metallic ring of a boulder as it breaks from its place of origin to bounce downward over the granite, or the deeper roar of a full-scale rock avalanche; the far scream of a hawk as it circles overhead; the tinkle of a rivulet; the splash of a leaping trout in some quiet lake; the stillness which is no sound at all but which at times pervades the High Country. Nor can odors be ignored, for who can forget the smell of a mountain morning—the pungence of pine needles in the heat of midday; the freshness that follows an afternoon shower; the odor of wood smoke at twilight. And the feel—of a mountain breeze; the warmth of sun by day and of campfire by night; the softness of a wooded trail under foot. Even taste, for there is nothing to compare with trout fried over an open fire, of biscuits baked in a reflector oven, or of beans cooked in an iron pot deep in the coals. These things are all part of your mountain experience and no description would be complete

without them. They are, indeed, *the* description—the essence of your High Adventure.

More and more people each year are enjoying these experiences for the first time, and these new people, added to those who return each season, give a sizeable and steadily increasing population to the back country. While there is no way to obtain an accurate count, the National Park Service estimates that at least 12,700 individuals traveled the trails of Kings Canyon National Park in 1962. People are discovering the back country, finding that they prefer it to the more crowded sections of the park.

In the general section at the beginning of this book, you will find a discussion of how best to enjoy the High Country. What is said there applies more or less to all Western parks containing mountain wilderness, and it is suggested that you reread this section before actually planning a vacation in Kings Canyon National Park.

Only you can decide what you want to do in the High Country. The time available, your physical condition, and the state of your finances all govern that decision. Prerequisite to any planning is the purchase of a topographic map. By studying it, you will see that network of trails covers the area. There are eleven trail entrances to this park exclusive of the many trails that cross the common boundary between Kings Canyon and Sequoia. With such an elaborate trail system, it is, of course, possible to enter at any one of the eleven points and eventually visit any spot you wish; but this is not the efficient way to explore the High Country.

To assist in your planning, therefore, four of the more popular trail entrances that can be approached by car will be discussed here. With the exception of Cedar Grove, all of these entrances are on the eastern side of the park. A few trips and certain points of interest are suggested for each of the entrances. They are primarily for the newcomer. Visitors who have spent several seasons in the area will probably wish to strike out on their own. It should be remembered that Kings Canyon contains hundreds of spots of outstanding grandeur, that it is a tremendous country where travel is slow, and that it will take many vacations to cover it with any degree of thoroughness.

Kings Canyon
Probably more people start into these mountains from Cedar Grove in the canyon of the Kings River than from any other point. The reason for this is probably

RIGHT
Southern climax *of Muir Trail is shown in this aerial photograph. Here, trail skirts Upper Rae Lake, disappears over Glen Pass, climbs to Forester Pass and Mt. Whitney*

PHOTO BY CLYDE SUNDERLAND

Mount Williamson

Kearsarge Pass

Mount Whitney

Forester Pass

Kearsarge Pinnacles

Mount Ericsson

Kern Canyon

Mount Kaweah

because one of the park's two developed areas is near the beginning of the trail. There are three routes you can take from the floor of Kings Canyon. **The Copper Creek Trail** to Granite Pass and Simpson Meadow starts at the big parking area at Roads End and heads due north up Copper Creek. Unless you are in good condition, this trip would be a tough one to start on if you are walking, so you had better let the horses do the work. It is a steady climb from the parking area (5,000 feet) to Granite Basin (10,000 feet), and the distance is around 12 miles. There are some nice views as you climb out of the canyon, but for the most part the scenery is not outstanding until you reach Granite Basin—roughly halfway to Simpson Meadow. Here you begin to see great expanses of bare granite and many little lakes. You should find good fishing in most of the lakes from here on. Granite Pass is at the far end of the Basin and is only 600 feet higher. From the pass, the route is comparatively level or downhill to Simpson Meadow, and much of the trip is through wooded country. Almost every back country traveler visits Simpson Meadow at one time or another. You should plan to spend at least two days here in this lovely spot on the Middle Fork of the Kings River a few miles above beautiful Blue Canyon and Tehi-piti Valley. There is a summer ranger station here and headquarters for a trail crew. Plan a week by horse for this trip—two days on the trail each way and two or three days at the Meadow.

Another trail which you should consider from Roads End is the **Paradise Valley Trail** which continues up the main river from the Copper Creek parking area. If you want a beautiful circle trip (four days by horse or a week backpacking) through the Sixty Lakes Basin-Rae Lakes-Charlotte Lake Country, you can take this trail one way and the Bubbs Creek Trail from the east end of the Kings Canyon the other way. The entire trip is about 43 miles, and there are a dozen spots where you can spend extra time. From the parking area, there is a climb of 1,500 feet up the South Fork and past Mist Falls to Paradise Valley. It is not a difficult climb, and the trail is well traveled. A level trail leads through the long, narrow valley to within about a mile of the mouth of Woods Creek. From here on, you gradually climb some 4,000 feet into the Rae Lake country which will be described later when we discuss the Kearsarge Pass entrance. The Paradise Valley and Woods Creek portions of this loop trip are delightful since the

trail is along the stream much of the way and there is fairly good fishing in the deep pools. You will find many ideal camping spots in the tiny meadows and in the wooded sections through which the route passes.

The third and by far the most popular trail out of the Kings Canyon is the **Bubbs Creek Trail.** From the parking area at Roads End, follow up either side of the river to the mouth of Bubbs Creek, about 2 miles distant. A bridge here enables you to cross from the north side of the river where you will hit the trail up the creek. This trail, like Paradise Valley Trail, leads into the Charlotte Lake and Rae Lakes Country—about three days round trip backpacking or a long two days by horse. For backpackers, Junction Meadow at the mouth of East Creek is far enough for the first day, and with an early start the next morning you should reach Charlotte Lake by noon. It is a cool trail, mostly through the woods. The long climb up Bubbs Creek is gradual except for the last 2 miles.

Kearsarge Pass

This approach is classed as one of the easiest entrances to the High Country from the east side. Ask at Independence for the road to Onion Valley, which is the trail head. The

Trail map of Kings Canyon and Sequoia back country shows John Muir Trail as it edges close to highest summits. Broken lines on map show trails that crisscross area

road is about 10 miles in length and climbs nearly 5,000 feet to its terminus (8,800 feet). There is a pack base here where animals may be rented and from which the pack trains start into the High Country. The trail is good, but there is little shade. It follows Pine Creek for part of the way and passes four small lakes so there is plenty of water. There will also be plenty of company since this is one of the most popular approaches from the east. The trail is a little over 4 miles in length to the top of the pass.

The trail drops a little over 1,000 feet to Bullfrog Lake 2 miles away. This basin is popular because it is a junction point of several trails. It contains the Kearsarge Lakes, Bullfrog Lake, and Charlotte Lake, all of which are within a radius of 1½ miles. There are many fine campsites in this area, however, firewood is somewhat scarce and the fishing is generally not too good.

This basin can be the starting point of many trips both long and short. A brisk climb of about 1,000 feet will take you to Glen Pass, on the John Muir Trail 1½ miles

Noisy and boisterous, *the Middle Fork of Kings River tumbles from its canyons to join forces with South Fork*

to the north. The pass is the gateway to the famous Rae Lakes-Sixty Lakes Basin country which lies at its northern base. Rae Lakes stretch for over a mile in a long narrow valley in the middle of which rises Fin Dome, a never-to-be-forgotten landmark. Beyond Rae Lakes lies a series of smaller lakes which are a part of the headwaters of the South Fork of Woods Creek. The whole valley is beautiful, with scattered clumps of trees and lots of water. Because it is on one of the main trails of the park, it is well patronized and, while there are plenty of campsites, you may find wood scarce and fishing not what you had hoped. The Sixty Lakes Basin lies directly over the 500-foot ridge that forms the western wall of the valley. Since this region is off the main trail, it is not so heavily used as the Rae Lakes Valley. The basin is dotted by many small sparkling lakes, fishing is fairly good, and there are plenty of attractive spots to camp.

For another good trip from the Charlotte Lake area follow the main trail south for about 1½ miles to Vidette Meadows. Then leave the trail and follow up Vidette Creek to the beautiful lakes of the same name which lie

in a granite basin between East and West Vidette Peaks. You can make this round trip in one day. An excellent trip which will take a day each way takes you into the Gardiner Lakes Basin at the foot of Mount Gardiner to the northwest. The trail follows the outlet of Charlotte Lake for about a mile and then begins a long and scenic climb of about 1,000 feet to a pass which overlooks the basin. You will not find many people here, for this area is well off the main-traveled routes. You'll find golden trout in the lakes.

If you would like a longer trip, you can use the Bullfrog Lake area as a starting point for the loop trip described under the Paradise Valley Trail out of Cedar Grove, going either down Bubbs Creek or over Glen Pass and down Woods Creek.

Taboose Pass

The road to the trail over **Taboose Pass** leaves U.S. Highway 6-395 about 14 miles north of Independence, ending some 6 miles away on the north side of Taboose Creek. The Taboose Pass entrance is probably the least popular of the four which are described in this book—probably because of the rugged 7-mile climb from the end of the road to the pass. In this distance, you climb 6,200 feet, and it is not until the trail crosses Taboose Creek at the 8,500-foot level that water is available. This trail is a rough one for pack stock, but they can be taken over it without too much difficulty. After crossing Taboose Creek, the trail becomes more scenic, and you will long remember the view from the pass into the South Fork of the Kings River. After another 2 miles and a descent of about 700 feet, you join the John Muir Trail, the main thoroughfare in the High Country. Nearby, intersecting the John Muir Trail from the west, is the trail that comes in from Cartridge Pass and the Simpson Meadow country beyond.

Fascinating country radiates out in all directions from the junction of these trails, and you can explore quite a distance in several directions on practically level ground. The long climb over the pass is forgotten, and you know that the return trip will be downhill with the exception of the first 700 feet. You can easily spend a week here exploring and fishing the many lakes and the network of streams.

About a mile south on the John Muir Trail, the trail to Bench Lake cuts to the west. This scenic trip of 2½ miles runs along the rim of the valley of the South Fork of the Kings. Bench Lake is a beautiful body of water perched at the far end of a long level plateau. It is a popular spot with those who know this section and you probably won't be alone, but the lake is large and there are plenty of scenic camping sites.

Another fine trip from the trail junction mentioned

above takes you south along the John Muir Trail again but continues on past the Bench Lake Trail to Lake Marjorie. This beautiful lake is situated in a long, comparatively level basin, with other smaller lakes both above and below it. The short trip of about 2½ miles is well worth the time. If you are feeling ambitious when you reach Lake Marjorie, continue on for another 2 miles to the top of Pinchot Pass. This is a climb of less than 1,000 feet, and only the last part is really strenuous. Your extra effort will be rewarded by the spectacular view into the headwaters of Woods Creek.

Back again at the trail junction, go north on the John Muir Trail for a mile and you will find yourself at the lower end of a delightful glacial basin 2 or 3 miles long which is dotted with small lakes connected by many small streams. Attractive campsites are plentiful, especially at the lower end where there is more timber. If you spend a couple of days exploring this area, you will probably want to see what is beyond Mather Pass at the basin's northern end. A zig zag trail leads to the top of the pass and, although long, it climbs less than 500 feet. From the top, you can look north into the headwaters of Palisade Creek and to North and Middle Palisade Peaks beyond. To the southeast, dominating the basin from which you have climbed, is Split Mountain (also known as the South Palisade.) All three of these peaks rise to over 14,000 feet.

Bishop Pass

The **Bishop Pass** entrance is one of the most beautiful of the eastern approaches to the High Country of Kings Canyon National Park. Not only is the trail to the pass outstanding, but the country beyond, containing the famous Evolution Valley in the northern section of the park, is a favorite among those who know the Sierra best.

Inquire at Bishop for the road up Bishop Creek to South Lake. There are some steep grades, but you should have no trouble. About 14 miles from Bishop, above the power plant of the Southern Sierra Power Company, take the left fork of the road to its terminus 7 miles above the fork and about 21 miles from Bishop. Accommodations and supplies may be obtained at two points in this last 7 miles—at Andrews Camp Lodge 5 or 6 miles below the end of the road, and at Rainbow Lodge, known to old timers as Parcher's Camp Lodge, at South Lake, the end of the road. Horses, pack animals, and guide service are also available. You can spend the night at either of these points and get an early start for the pass the next morning.

The trail over Bishop Pass starts at South Lake, elevation 9,750 feet. You travel 7 miles to the top of the pass, and you climb 2,250 feet in getting there; but the ascent is a gradual one except for a short steep section just before you reach the pass. The scenery along this route is outstanding. Beginning with South Lake, a chain of sparkling lakes extends almost to the summit. These lie in a great glacial cirque hemmed in by towering cliffs and peaks.

From Bishop Pass a 2-mile trail drops about 700 feet to Dusy Lakes. This is the first good place to camp, and the several lakes in this basin are worth exploring. You might wish to try some fishing here. Less than a mile farther, the trail passes the lower end of another small basin which also contains several small lakes.

Three miles beyond Dusy Lakes, the trail intersects the John Muir Trail which comes down from the Evolution Valley country. By turning right and going up the John Muir Trail for a half a mile, you come to Little Pete Meadow, a favorite stopping point for trail parties. However, by going another half mile beyond, you will reach another small meadow south of the trail where you will find more wood and probably fewer people than at Little Pete Meadow. Try fishing the stream, which is the Middle Fork of the Kings.

What you do from this point depends upon your own inclinations. An easy trip of 7 miles down the John Muir Trail (south), past Grouse Meadow and up Palisade Creek, brings you to beautiful Deer Meadow where there is plenty of wood, water, fish, and scenery. You can spend a lot of time here, either being lazy or getting a workout by following the trail farther toward Mather Pass.

If Deer Meadow doesn't appeal to you, go up the trail (north). It is a 6-mile trip to Muir Pass and you climb nearly 3,000 feet in that distance; but it is a trip you will not forget. You can camp at several small lakes, but the higher you go, the less wood you will find. It is not an easy 6 miles to the pass, but once at the top you are at the gateway to the famous Evolution Country and some of the most spectacular scenery in the Sierra. At the pass you will find a stone shelter built by the Sierra Club in memory of John Muir. It is for the use of anyone who is caught on the pass in a storm. You will probably find a supply of wood but don't use it unless you have to, and if you do use it, replenish the supply for those who will follow you.

It would not be feasible here to map trails that should be taken in the country beyond Muir Pass. This is a big country, and you can spend weeks exploring it. Parts of it are rugged, barren and harsh as the granite of which it is composed, yet there is beauty in this ruggedness. And parts of it are filled with another kind of beauty—the soft beauty of delightful meadows, singing streams, and sparkling lakes. I often wonder if Emerson Hough was not thinking particularly of the Evolution Country when he said there was no comparable place on earth.

Lassen Volcanic National Park

Lassen's 1915 eruption *flattened trees, left them lying pointed away from the source of the blast. Devastated northeast side is now undergoing natural reforestation*

How to Get There

By Car: Lassen is California's only national park that can be entered from both sides without having to cross a high pass. By consulting the map, you will see that there are four ways to enter the park. One road comes in at the northeast corner and leads to Butte Lake; one from the south goes to Drakesbad; and the main Lassen Park road, connects State Route 89, at the Southwest Entrance on the southwest with the Manzanita Lake Entrance on the northwest.

By Train, Bus, and Air: The Southern Pacific Railroad serves Red Bluff and Redding, and the Western Pacific Railroad stops at Keddie. Concessioner buses will meet trains at Redding and transport you to the park during the operating season.

Redding, Red Bluff, and Susanville are served by commercial bus lines, and connecting transportation by the concessioner is available to Manzanita Lake from Redding during the operating season. Commercial bus transportation is available the year around from Red Bluff and Susanville to Mineral where, during the summer, arrangements can be made for the concessioner to pick you up and take you through the park to Manzanita Lake.

The nearest commercial airports are located at Redding and Red Bluff. During the summer season, concession buses will meet planes.

Note: If you want transportation to the park be sure to advise the company well in advance. Write the Lassen National Park Company, Manzanita Lake, California.

Where to Stay

Accommodations are provided by the concessioner, the Lassen National Park Company. There are only two places to stay in the park: Manzanita Lake Lodge, located in the northwest corner on the main road, and Drakesbad, in the southern part of the park and reached over a secondary road from Chester.

Manzanita Lake Lodge is the largest, best-equipped, and most comfortable place to stay in Lassen. The main rustic building contains a lobby, a curio section, cocktail lounge, and dining room. The meals are above average, attractively served, and reasonably priced.

The Lodge has a variety of cabins, tents, and cottages, ranging from $8.00 to $11.00 for one, and from $9.00 to $12.00 for two. Most luxurious are the hotel bungalow bedrooms; most economical the standard bedrooms. For a family (limited to 6 persons) that wishes the best in housekeeping accommodations, the Pine Cottages offer excellent facilities for $21.00 a day. These contain a bed-room with double beds, a sitting room with a hideaway bed, and a kitchen equipped with an electric range and refrigerator as well as all cooking utensils and a table setting for four. If you prefer something less expensive, lower-priced housekeeping type cabins are available.

Drakesbad Guest Ranch is the place to go if you aren't looking for people, because accommodations here are limited to fifty. It's quiet and restful and the kind of place where everyone knows everyone else within a few hours of their arrival. Facilities are a little more primitive here than at Manzanita Lake.

The main building contains attractive hotel rooms and lobby, and there are also furnished cottages with modern plumbing and heat.

Drakesbad usually opens a little later and closes a few days earlier than Manzanita. It operates on American Plan, and a room for two in the main building or in a cabin will cost $12.00 each. Children from 4 to 7 are entitled to half rate unless occupying separate rooms.

Free Government Campgrounds are well distributed throughout the park. Some have modern conveniences, while others are rustic and undeveloped. Among the eight which have been established, you will certainly be able to find one that suits your own individual taste. Manzanita is the only one within walking distance of a store and post office. All campgrounds in the park have a 14-day limit.

Manzanita Lake Campground, with 275 campsites, is located near the east end of Manzanita Lake. It is well equipped (and well patronized) and has outdoor tables and benches, fireplaces with iron grates, tap water, flush toilets, and electric razor outlets. Uncut wood for your fire is available. It is the only place in the Manzanita Lake area where trailers are permitted. This campground opens earlier and closes later than any of the others. Usually it is ready for occupancy about the first of May and does not close until the middle of October. Elevation at the campground is 5,890 feet.

Summit Lake Campground is a favorite with many who desire some conveniences and yet prefer smaller numbers of campers. There are 94 campsites here, and it is cooler than Manzanita since it is about 800 feet higher. Summit Lake isn't as large as Manzanita, but it is big enough for boating and swimming and some fishing—if you're lucky. The campground is divided into two sections, one on the south end of the lake and one on the north, each containing tables, uncut firewood, flush toilets, tap water and fireplaces. It is open from mid-June to mid-September, and house trailers are permitted. If your primary interest is hiking or riding, this is the place to stay. Many of the park trails start in this area, and corrals are nearby where riding and pack animals can be rented.

Kings Creek Campground (16 miles from Manzanita, 22 from Mineral) is the highest in the park and, because of its altitude (7,150 feet) it retains a snow cover late. You shouldn't plan to camp here much before the 10th of July or after Labor Day. You will find the days cooler here than at the lower camps and some of the nights are chilly; so come prepared. There are only 18 campsites and accommodations for small trailers. Fireplaces, tables, pit toilets are provided, but there are no water taps. Water is taken from the stream. Although there is no lake, it is a beautiful spot.

Southwest Campground is located at an altitude of 6,700 feet, about half a mile inside the Southwest Entrance Station. It is small, with only 16 campsites. It has piped water, pit toilets, tables, and fireplaces.

Butte Lake Campground is rather isolated but is restful and popular with those who like it because of good fishing in the lake and its proximity to Cinder Cone. Campers who know the park well consider this the best campground. There is swimming in nearby Bathtub Lake, and there are boats for rent at Butte. The campground has all the regular facilities including piped water in its 30 campsites. There is a ranger station there and an emergency telephone. Drive 18 miles on State Rt. 44 from Old Station. Then take the 6-mile dirt road leading south from 44 to the campground (this is not advisable for trailers). The campground is at an elevation of 6,100 feet and is open from about the first of June to mid-October. Nearest supplies are at Old Station, where there is also a post office.

Warner Valley Campground is on the road to Drakesbad. In fact, it is only a mile from the resort; so if you get tired of cooking, you can go up to the ranch for a meal. The campground is fairly small, with only 15 campsites with room for small trailers. Water is piped, and there are pit toilets as well as the usual tables and fireplaces. In addition, it is within easy hiking distance of the nearby thermal area where you'll see Boiling Springs Lake, Terminal Geyser (which isn't one), and the Devil's Kitchen. All in all it is a pleasant campground, with fairly good stream fishing and not too many people.

Don't try to take your trailer beyond the campground as the road is fairly steep and you may have trouble. If you expect mail, have it addressed c/o Warner Valley Ranger Station, Chester, California. The ranger station is a mile from the campground. A phone is located at Drakesbad. This campground is low—5,650 feet—and is open from about June 1 to October 1.

Juniper Lake Campground is on the south shore of the lake about 16 miles from Chester, reached by a dirt road that is generally rough in spots. It is higher than Warner Valley (6,745 feet) and is open from mid-June to October 1. There are 12 campsites here but no space for trailers.

Outdoor tables, fireplaces, and pit toilets are provided, but it's necessary to use lake water *which should be boiled*. You can swim and fish in the lake. Fishing is fair to good in this and other lakes in the vicinity. There are several good hiking trails, one of which leads to the top of Mt. Harkness with its fire lookout. It is only about a 1,300 foot climb on a trail about 1½ miles long.

Horseshoe Lake Campground is less than two miles beyond Juniper and is slightly lower. It has some advantages over Juniper which may make it worth your while to go on. For one thing, water comes from springs and doesn't have to be boiled, and fireplaces are provided. There is also a fire control station here with an emergency telephone. You cannot take a house trailer into this camp, and even some boat trailers are not recommended. No motors are permitted on this or any other park lake. Fishing is about the same as indicated for Juniper, and the season is the same.

If you are staying at Horseshoe or Juniper campgrounds, have your mail addressed to the campground c/o General Delivery, Chester.

There are organizational campgrounds available for organized groups with room for about 200 persons. The camps are furnished with large fireplaces for cooking, and, of course, tables and pit toilets. Stream water may be used. Although the facilities are a little primitive, these spots are ideal for groups that want to be by themselves and organize their own programs.

Facilities Available

The Naturalist Program at Lassen is extensive, considering that it is one of the smaller parks, and you will find it of high quality. Evening illustrated talks are given at the Manzanita Amphitheater, which is within easy walking distance of the lodge and the adjacent campground. Similar talks are given at the Summit Lake Campground.

The Visitor Center at Manzanita Lake is most attractive and contains excellent exhibits on thermal phenomena, Indians, human and natural history. A feature which both adults and youngsters will enjoy is the Indian program which is given twice daily 6 days a week. Across the road from the Visitor Center is the fine Lily Pond Nature Trail that partly circles Reflection Lake. There are four other self-guiding nature trails at Lassen—Bumpass Hell, Sulphur Works, Boiling Springs Lake in the Drakesbad area and Cinder Cone.

Short, two-hour nature walks, half-day trips, and the trip up Lassen Peak are offered several times each week by the naturalist staff. These trips originate at the Visitor Center.

(cont. on next page)

LASSEN FACTUAL INFORMATION

Medical Facilities are lacking here. The nearest ones are at Redding, Red Bluff, Burney, and Chester.

Service Clubs are also lacking locally, and you will have to go to Redding, Red Bluff, Burney, or Chester.

Church Services, both Catholic and Protestant, are held each Sunday during the season at Manzanita Lake and Mineral.

Baby Sitting: There is no "organized" baby sitting at Lassen, but generally one of the college girls who works there in the summer will be glad to pick up a little extra money in her off-hours. For information, inquire at the desk in the Lodge.

Supplies can be obtained at Viola, Mineral, Childs Meadows Resort, Manzanita Lake, and at Old Station about 15 miles outside the Manzanita Lake Entrance. During the season these stores are pretty well stocked with fresh vegetables, fruit, milk, etc.

Meals, Fountain, and Cocktail Service: Meals can be obtained at the Lodge and at Drakesbad and at the lunch and soda counter in the Manzanita Lake store. Although the store is open from 8 A.M. to 8 P.M., the grill and lunch counter are open only from 10 A.M. to 6 P.M. Cocktails are served in the Crater Room, located in the basement of the Lodge.

Horse Rental: The corrals are located near Summit Lake, since this area is centrally situated and is more or less a trail hub.

Swimming and Boating are both popular at Lassen. Boats are for rent at Manzanita and Butte Lakes for $2.50 half day or $4.00 all day, or you can haul your own boat in and launch it on most of the accessible lakes. However *no motors* are permitted in the park. Swimming is enjoyed at both Manzanita and Summit. In fact, you can swim in most of the lakes, although you may find some of them too cold. There is a warm-water pool at Drakesbad which is free to guests of the Guest Ranch.

Mail and Telephone: There is a post office in the General Store at Manzanita Lake and mail should be sent there c/o General Delivery unless you are staying at one of the two resorts. If you are staying at one of the outlying campgrounds, you will get better service by addressing it as suggested under "Campgrounds" in this section. There is telephone and telegraph service at Manzanita Lake Lodge and at Drakesbad, and there are emergency intra-park telephones scattered throughout the park, at the entrances, and at ranger stations.

Laundry: At Manzanita Lake you will find self-service laundry and drying facilities. Inquire about this at the Lodge desk.

Ice can be bought at the General Store at Manzanita Lake or outside the park.

Gas and Oil can be had at the filling station near the General Store. Minor repairs can be handled here and more extensive service is available at Mineral.

Pets are permitted but must be kept under physical restraint at all times. They are not allowed on trails. No kennel service is available.

Fishing

In general, fishing is good at Lassen, especially in the spring and fall, and this is one area where you don't have to go too far to get fish. The limit is 10 pounds or ten fish except in Manzanita and Reflection Lakes where it is 5 pounds or 5 fish. A California State license is required and can be purchased at the Lodge.

Lassen is one of the exceptions to the rule that you can't drive your car to the fish. There are several lakes and streams accessible by car where fishing is fairly good at certain seasons, especially September and October.

The rainbow trout is the only native fish, but the waters have been stocked with Eastern brook and brown trout. Some of the lakes are barren and cannot support fish; so to save time and disappointment, consult a ranger or naturalist about them.

Manzanita Lake is probably fished more than any other lake in the park and yet fishermen continue to catch fish there. It is stocked with browns (there are some big ones) and rainbows. You can fish either from the bank or rent a boat. Try flies, especially in the evening.

Reflection Lake is just across the road from Manzanita and conditions are about the same except the fish will generally run smaller. Try working the west shore, again in the evening.

Horseshoe Lake contains many rainbows averaging a pound or more. It is best to fish from a boat; but if you did not trail one in, try flies or bait along the east shore.

Snag Lake is 3½ miles by trail from Horseshoe Lake. It has never been too good for flies, but some fine catches have been made with "hardware." The rainbows average 3 pounds and are taken mostly from the north and west shores.

Bluff Lakes—there are two of them about a mile southwest of Horseshoe, and you will find plenty of Eastern brooks that like flies better than spinners.

Soda Lake is a hike of a couple of miles from the highway and is reached by crossing the saddle between Eagle Peak and Ski Heil. You should get Eastern brooks and rainbows on spinners and streamer flies, but if you don't the scenery is well worth the trip.

Dersch Meadows (East Fork of Hat Creek) is just off the highway east of the Devastated Area. The rainbows and Eastern brooks are small but plentiful. In nearby Hat Lake, in 1953, a 32-inch German brown weighing nearly 15 pounds was brought to net. He has become a legend, so try your luck and see if there aren't more of the big ones.

Lower Hat Creek is reached by a dirt road from the Devastated Area. Follow it until you are about a mile below the second bridge and then hike a half mile outside the park. It used to be, and probably still is, loaded with small rainbows that love flies.

LASSEN VOLCANIC NATIONAL PARK is small enough to give you a feeling of intimacy, large enough to give you plenty of exercise on foot or horseback, and different enough to pique the curiosity of even the most blasé visitor. Furthermore, the visitor does not feel the pressure of crowds that he may experience at Yosemite Valley or at Giant Forest in Sequoia. The tempo of summer activity at Lassen seems more leisurely than in many parks —people take things easier and enjoy themselves equally as much. It is an area of charming diversification both in activities and in natural features.

Lassen is a park, of course, by virtue of the comparatively recent eruptions of Lassen Peak which has the distinction of being the most recently active volcano in the United States, exclusive of those in Alaska and Hawaii. A miniature Yellowstone without the geysers, Lassen has hot springs and pools, steam vents and fumaroles, mud pots and cinder cones, as well as large expanses that have been denuded as a result of the volcanic action.

But there is more than this—much more. There are isolated lakes and singing streams where you will find good fishing. Beautiful trails lead to out-of-the-way places, over mountain meadows lush with wildflowers in late spring and through dense coniferous forests and friendly groves of quaking aspen with their fresh green leaves.

The main roads are smooth, the trails are good, the accommodations are comfortable, and the weather is usually perfect from June until late October. Each season at Lassen has its charms; but autumn, from Labor Day to the end of October, is especially delightful—Indian summer with deep blue skies, golden brown leaves, pleasantly warm days and crisp nights. Fishing improves from the first of September on and there are few people in the park. Manzanita Lake Lodge closes around September 20 and Drakesbad a few days earlier; but other spots such as Viola Resort, Mineral Lodge, Childs Meadows Resort, Fire Mountain Lodge, Deer Creek Lodge, and St. Bernard Lodge are within easy driving distance and most of them are open the year around.

Whatever it is you are looking for—hiking, riding, swimming, fishing, photography, scenery or just plain loafing—whether you are camping or availing yourself of Lassen's accommodations, you'll like the friendly, intimate feeling one experiences in California's northernmost national park.

History

History does not record the name of the first white man to enter what is now Lassen Volcanic National Park, or even who first saw its hot pools and steaming valleys. We can surmise, however, that it was someone from one of the

THEODORE OSMUNDSON

Local Indian woman *shows visitors basket-making techniques, while Ranger-naturalist explains Indian history. These demonstrations are features of naturalist program*

various emigrant parties that headed into northern California during the late 1840's and early 1850's.

Lassen Peak itself was named for Peter Lassen, a Danish immigrant and early pioneer in the region, who conducted parties from Humboldt, Nevada, into the Sacramento Valley for a few years beginning in 1848. Legend has it Lassen was not too skilled a guide, that he frequently became lost himself, and that the so-called Lassen Trail, which passed within six miles of the present park area, was anything but a direct route. Some historians say that Peter used Lassen Peak for a landmark one day and Mount Shasta the next, and never really knew the difference. There is also an interesting yarn that once when Lassen became lost, the group that he was guiding forced him at gunpoint to climb the peak which now bears his name in order to get his correct location. If this tale is true, it is possible that he was actually the first white man to enter the park area; but if it is not true, his only connection with the park is that he used the peak as a landmark. During that time the peak was always known as St. Joseph's

Rockslides from Chaos Crags, *riding on slippery base of wet volcanic ash, raced across level ground—and even* *uphill—to form nearly impassable Chaos Jumbles. The Jumbles cover area approximately 2½ square miles in size*

Mountain, and it was not until 1856 that the name Lassen Peak was first recorded in print.

By 1850 well-founded rumors began to circulate about the uncertainties and hazards of the Lassen Trail. Fewer and fewer travelers elected to take it, and the emigrant-hungry settlements in northern California began to suffer.

Promotion methods really haven't changed much since that time and the businessmen of these settlements did exactly what businessmen today would do under similar circumstances. To lure the emigrants, they had a new route laid out which was admittedly much better and shorter than the Lassen Trail. This new route, known as the Nobles Pass Trail, ran between Black Rock, Nevada, and Fort Reading, California (now Redding). It proved popular from the beginning and was used for many years. The Nobles Pass Trail entered what is now Lassen Park at Butte Lake in the northeast corner, traversed the northern section of the present park, and left it near Manzanita Lake. Probably it was a party of emigrants on this trail that witnessed and reported the 1851 eruption of Cinder Cone.

Although overgrown in places with chaparral, the old trail is still visible today and, in fact, part of it is used by National Park Service vehicles on official business.

After the emigration activities dwindled in northern California, nothing of important historical significance occurred within the confines of the park until the eruptions of Lassen Peak beginning in 1914 subsequently led to the establishment of the national park in 1916.

The Indians

During your Lassen visit, you will see Indian exhibits in the museum and you can also attend the Indian Lore Program which is given twice daily. Here you can learn much of the habits and customs of the local Indians.

No battles were fought, no emigrant trains were attacked and burned, no settlers were murdered—in fact, nothing relating to the Indians occurred within Lassen's present boundaries that would make even a fair television program. The park area was, however, the meeting ground of four tribes—the Atsugewi, Yana, Yahi, and Mountain Maidu. These four tribes combined are estimated to have had a population of 4,025 in 1770, but by 1950 this number had dwindled to 350.

Lassen was a summer camping, hunting, and fishing ground for the Indians. They came in the spring, following the deer to the higher elevations, and remained until late fall when they returned to their more permanent homes in the valleys and foothills. Since it was more or less common ground, all four tribes used the area and

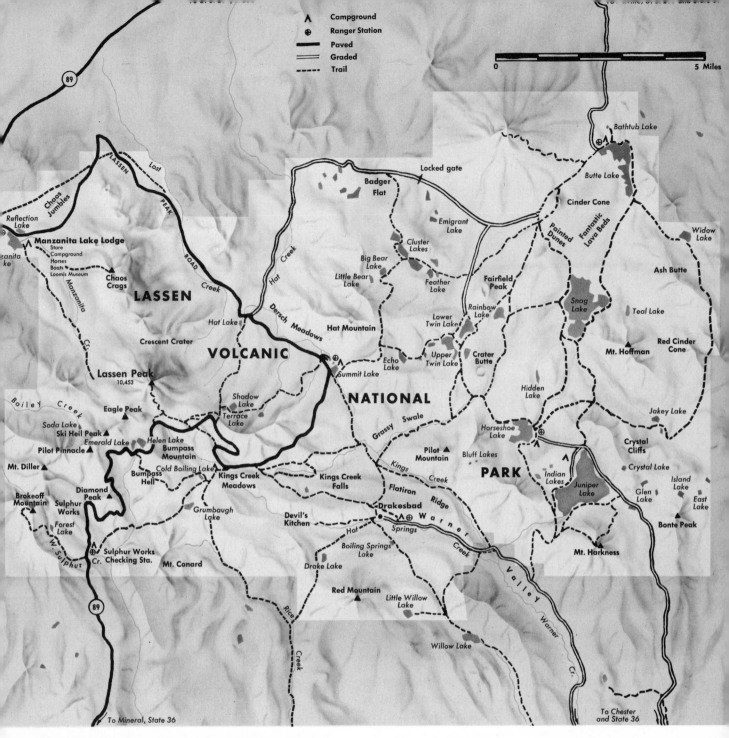

appear to have gotten along together in a fairly peaceful manner, even to the extent of intermarrying on occasion.

Their habits and customs were similar—that of a simple peace-loving hill and mountain people. A few of the descendants of these Indians still live in the vicinity of the park.

Interesting as are the life, beliefs, and customs of these early people, there is an even more fascinating tale. It is the story of the last survivor of the Yahi Tribe who called himself Ishi, which means simply, "I am a man."

In 1910 it was estimated that only five members of the Yahi Tribe remained. They were in a completely wild state and had been seen but once. Then, in 1916, a half-starved, emaciated creature, whose only clothing was a torn piece of canvas over his shoulders, was "captured" near a slaughter house in the vicinity of Oroville. He spoke in a tongue no one had ever heard and, in spite of his condition, refused food and remained huddled in the corner of a cell where a sheriff had locked him. Here he might have died had not word reached the department of

JOHN ROBINSON

Impressive Lassen Peak *dominates landscape from almost any point in vicinity. It stands at the southern end of the Cascade Range and rises 10,457 feet above sea level*

anthropology at the University of California about "The Wild Man of Oroville," a name which had been given him by a newspaper reporter with a flair for the sensational. Excitedly following a hunch, an anthropologist left posthaste for Oroville. If his hunch were correct, the "wild man" was the most remarkable anthropological discovery in years, for he could be the lone living representative of a people thought to be extinct and of whom not too much was known.

The professor's job was difficult at best and it was further complicated by the fact that no one knew the Yahi language. His only aid was a list of words from the vocabulary of a people known to be the closest relatives of the Yahi. Patiently, he went through the list and finally he hit a word that brought a delighted response from Ishi. From this beginning the professor gained the Indian's confidence to such an extent that he was finally able to take him to Berkeley. Ishi was given quarters at the Museum of Anthropology where he did simple tasks for the $25 a month which he was paid.

Ishi died of tuberculosis five years later, but during that period he made many friends among the museum staff and contributed a great amount of information about a people of which he was the last survivor.

You will find the detailed story of Ishi in a book, *Ishi in Two Worlds,* by Theodora Kroeber (widow of Dr. Kroeber who "sponsored" Ishi at the Museum of Anthropology), which was published in 1961 and has been widely acclaimed.

The Story Of A Volcano

There is no reason to complicate the story of Lassen Peak by trying to tell the geological history of the Cascade Range. Suffice to say, the Cascades are volcanic in origin, and such well-known peaks as Baker, Rainier, Adams, Hood, Shasta, Lassen, and others are all old volcanos of which Lassen is the most recently active. It is also the southernmost of the major Cascade peaks that poured forth their lavas and formed a link in the great Pacific Circle of Fire—a chain of volcanoes which ring the Pacific Ocean.

Lassen Peak itself is the child of a much greater volcano—the ancestral Mount Tehama which geologists tell us was over a thousand feet higher than Lassen Peak, measured fifteen miles across the base, and had a crater, 3,000 feet in diameter. Upon the flank of this great volcano, Lassen Peak came into being, first as a small crater from which flowed more and more lava piling ever higher until the present mountain was formed. Then, as if satisfied that its offspring could carry on by itself, tired old Mount Tehama collapsed, probably because of a lack of support from beneath. If you have an eye for geological landscapes, you can still see remnants of Tehama's flank in Brokeoff Mountain, Mount Diller, and Pilot Pinnacle.

Until May 30, 1914, Lassen Peak was known principally as a landmark Peter Lassen had used in the early days to guide emigrants into the Sacramento Valley. For those who lived within sight of it, it was just another peak—beautiful, of course, and the highest in that section

This early photograph *of Lassen Peak was taken during 1915 eruptions. Energy of volcano was largely spent by end of 1915 but some activity continued*

of the country, but just another peak. It had been quiescent for a long, long time—certainly longer than white men had lived in America—although there was evidence that one or more mud flows had come down the slopes within the last 500 years.

But on May 30, 1914, it became more than just another mountain. Things began to happen which were ultimately to change the face of the peak and to bring the area into national prominence. That day marked the beginning of a series of year-long eruptions of smoke, stones, gas, and ash that culminated in the awesome spectacle of May 19, 1915.

These began when a great red column of lava rose in the crater and spilled over the sides melting the snow on the northeast slope and sending 20-ton boulders and devastating floods of warm mud down the valleys of Lost Creek and Hat Creek.

Three days later Lassen literally "blew its top." A column of vapor and ash rose over 5 miles in the air, photographs of which look for all the world like the mushroom cloud of a nuclear explosion. So powerful was the eruption that ashes were scattered as far away as Reno, Nevada, where the streets were covered with several inches of powdery debris. At the same time, a terrifying blast of steam and hot gas burst from the side of the peak and roared northeast, killing every living thing in its path and flattening all the trees. Today you can see the results of this blast in the Devastated Area where, by looking closely, you will observe the down trees all pointing in the same direction.

After this big blowoff, there were minor declining eruptions lasting into 1917, but Lassen's forces were spent.

All that remains today are a few wisps of steam rising from the crater. The white plume is visible on cool days.

An interesting feature some 10 airline miles from Lassen Peak is beautiful Cinder Cone near Butte Lake in the northeast corner of the park. It rises in artistic symmetry approximately 700 feet from the base and is another evidence of the terrifying pent-up forces that lay beneath the surface. Cinder cones are usually built rapidly over a period of a few years or a few decades. They are true volcanos, but are formed under conditions where the lava is so charged with gas and pressure that it is thrown out with great violence and literally explodes. While flying through the air, the tiny fragments of lava cool and fall as cinders.

The park abounds with evidence of dying volcanic activity. Hot springs, steam vents, and fumaroles persist for many years after eruptions have subsided. There are several such thermal areas in Lassen. The best known— probably because it is just off the road—is Sulphur Works, located a short distance inside the southwest entrance. About 5 miles further on is the beginning of a fine self-guiding trail which leads you through Bumpass Hell. In addition, you can see steam rising from Little Hot Springs Valley as you drive over the main road. There is a thermal area in Warner Valley within easy walking distance of Drakesbad. Here again you will find a self-guiding trail to Boiling Springs Lake. Terminal Geyser and Devil's Kitchen are also in the vicinity. There are other less important places in the park where there is some thermal activity, but the ones listed above are the best known and most frequently visited.

Some of the springs in the park are actually boiling

hot, but the agitation in most of them is due to hot gases rising through the water.

A word of caution here. Watch your step, keep on the trails, and don't go too near the edge of hot pools. The crust is thin in places and severe burns have resulted from people being too enthusiastic and too venturesome.

Two questions are frequently asked by first-time visitors to Lassen. Why are there hot springs here, and will the peak ever erupt again? The answer to the first question is simple—because the hot magmas and rocks are sufficiently near the surface to "keep the pot boiling." The answer to the second question is purely speculative—it might and it might not. If it were to let go again, however, it would give plenty of advance warning.

Trees And Flowers

Probably a greater percentage of Lassen's area is covered with vegetation than is true for any other California park. The reason for this is that less of it is above timberline.

At lower elevations you will find several pines—the Jeffrey, the ponderosa, the lodgepole, the western white and the sugar pine as well as the white fir. In the Manzanita Lake area there is some incense cedar and Douglas fir; and higher up, the red fir and the mountain hemlock. Still higher, even at timberline, are the white-barked pines, with their trunks often gnarled and twisted by the force of the wind. Cottonwood, alder, willow, and aspen, are all present, especially in moist situations, and part of the charm of Lassen's streams is the cool shade and the dancing sunlight and shadow that these trees contribute.

Chaparral is a general name given to the bushy growth that frequently covers the hillsides in California. At Lassen the chaparral is composed mainly of tobacco brush, chinquapin and manzanita. As you approach Manzanita Lake from the Devastated Area, you will see great treeless hillsides covered with dense thickets of manzanita, unmistakable for its oval leathery green leaves, red bark and, in the spring, its masses of small bright pink flowers.

Wildflowers are everywhere in Lassen from the water-loving orchids in the lakes to the drought-resistant varieties that live on the dry lava flows. There are several hundred species found in the park, and because of the deep snows and subsequent late spring in certain sections, one can enjoy a seasonal progression of flowers from early June to late September.

When it is spring, you will find Indian paintbrush, bleeding heart, monkey flowers, tiger lilies and a host of other blooms, many of which persist throughout the summer. The showy red snowplant is abundant—but remember the heavy fine both within and outside the park for disturbing one. In the higher mountain meadows, mountainheath, lupine and penstemon put on their finest display in mid-August.

The orange wallflower, the bog Kalmia, the senecios, the balsam roots, the marsh marigolds, the monkshood, the shooting stars, the dainty white rein orchid, and the blue false forget-me-not—these and hundreds more can be found at some season, and all do their part to add charm and color to the landscape.

Animals

You'll see one animal in Lassen that you may not find in any other California national park—the Columbian blacktail deer. You will also find your old friend the mule deer. Both are fairly common here.

The black bears, too, seem to have better manners. Although there are quite a few in the area, they are seen infrequently.

Ground squirrels and chipmunks are numerous. Pine squirrels or chickarees chatter from the trees, and if you keep your eyes open when you are in the wooded sections a distance away from the roads, you may be lucky enough to spot a pine marten. Sometimes, in the meadows along roads, you will be able to catch a glimpse of the beautiful red foxes that are not uncommon here. Marmots or western woodchucks are, of course, readily seen, especially at the higher elevations.

More than 100 species of birds have been identified in this park, ranging from several tiny humming birds to the big bald eagle. Lassen, with its abundant vegetation, meadows, lakes, and streams, is an ideal place for bird study, especially in fall. The various lakes seem alive with waterfowl, and some of the water-loving species such as

TOP
Mount Tehama's ancient cone *(shown by dotted line) is gone, leaving a ragged-rimmed basin. Brokeoff Mountain, Mt. Diller, Pilot Pinnacle are remnants of Tehama's flank*

BOTTOM LEFT
Boiling Springs Lake *is easily reached from Drakesbad via a self-guiding trail. Vapors rise from the surface but this fascinating lake is so clear you can see the bottom.*

BOTTOM RIGHT
At Sulphur Works, *the earth's reeking gases bubble up through the hot mud. This interesting thermal area is just off the highway near the Southwest Entrance Station*

JOHN ROBINSON

RICHARD DAWSON

The General Store *at Manzanita Lake is amply stocked with groceries and campers' supplies. You can buy curios here, and there is a lunch counter. The Manzanita Lake area in northwest corner of the park is center of activity*

the killdeer, the belted kingfisher, and the water ouzel are here most of the year. The beautiful mountain quail, and friendly mountain chickadee spend the year in the area. The same saucy Stellar jay that you have met in other California parks is in Lassen, ready and eager to share your meal, or even to steal it if you don't seem to be in a cooperative mood. Quite his equal in noise and impertinence is the Clark's nutcracker, a big gray bird with black wings.

Generally speaking, bird life here is not too different from that found in Yosemite or Sequoia, but it is interesting that so many kinds are found in an area so small and with an altitudinal range of only about 5,000 feet.

Points You Should See

One of the park's pleasant features is that you can sample many of its attractions without even getting out of your car, or by walking only a few hundred feet at the most.

One of the best ways to be sure that you miss nothing on the main road through the park is to purchase a copy of the booklet *Road Guide to the Lassen Volcanic National Park.* The text of this handy and interesting little book is keyed to numbered stakes set along the road. Some of the following points are covered in the guide, but some of them, because they are not on the main road, are not included.

Manzanita and Reflection Lakes

These two lakes are just inside the northwest boundary, one on each side of the highway. There is fishing, boating, and swimming; and if you are a photographer, you can snap some spectacular color pictures of Lassen Peak with Manzanita Lake in the foreground. The scene is especially beautiful when the first snows have mantled the peak and the foliage around the lake has turned to its blazing fall colors.

Don't miss the fine self-guiding nature trail (The Lily Pond Trail) that circles part of Reflection Lake and which

Manzanita Lake, *only a step from the Lodge and camp-grounds, is a popular spot for boating, swimming, fishing.* *You can rent boats or use your own, but no motors are permitted. You can catch both brown and rainbow trout here*

you can cover in less than an hour's easy stroll. It's not only pleasant but instructive as well.

The Visitor Center at Manzanita Lake

The exhibits here are outstanding, one of the best being the diorama which shows Lassen Peak before the eruption and which, by the press of a button, presents the peak as you see it today. Outside the Visitor Center is a seismograph station that records earthquakes. You can watch the delicate instruments through a big window.

Emerald Lake

The lake is about 7 miles from the Southwest Entrance Station and is a typical high mountain lake alongside the Lassen Park Road.

Bumpass Hell

The trail to Bumpass Hell, largest thermal area in the park, begins at the road near Emerald Lake. This is another self-guiding trail, which winds through a small basin filled with hot pools, steam vents, and fumeroles. If you have been to Yellowstone Park, Bumpass Hell will remind you of some of the basins there although it is on a smaller scale.

Sulphur Works

This is another thermal area right off the road a short distance inside the Southwest Entrance Station. It is smaller than Bumpass Hell, but it has some interesting features. There is a self-guiding trail, and a ranger naturalist is on duty daily from 8 A.M. to 5 P.M.

Butte Lake

A paved road, State 44, turns off Highway 89 a mile north of Old Station. Follow this road east for 18 miles then south 6 miles on a gravelled road which goes to Butte Lake in the northeast corner of the park. In addition to the lake, which has a character all its own, there is Cinder Cone less than two miles away. A good self-guiding trail runs from the lake to the Cone and winds through the fantastic lava beds laid down in the 1851 eruption. If you take this trail, be sure to go to the top of the Cone, for it is not only an experience to look down into the crater but the 700-foot height gives you a fine view of the surrounding lava flows.

The Drakesbad Area

A number of interesting thermal features can be reached by short walks from the Drakesbad resort. At Drakesbad pick up one of the free leaflets and follow it over the 2-mile self-guiding trail that takes you around Boiling Springs Lake. This trail first crosses a beautiful meadow and ascends gradually through a fine forest of lodgepole pine and red and white fir. It will take you through an area of trees that have been freshly killed by a recent extension of the thermal activity. The lake itself boils and bubbles with the action of sub-surface springs and steam vents, and the land around it roars and hisses with jets of escaping steam, and bubbles with large mud pots.

Subway Cave Lava Tube

Although outside the park, in Lassen National Forest, this feature is well worth seeing. It is reached by taking Highway 89 north about 15 miles beyond the Manzanita Lake Entrance, parking your car and walking a hundred feet or so. The tube is a long tunnel formed in one of

NATIONAL PARK SERVICE PHOTO

the big lava flows. The outside of the flow cooled and consolidated while the core was still liquid. The core drained, leaving the lava shell through which you can walk. About halfway between the park and the Lava Tube you will pass Big Spring on the right side of the road. Stop and watch the torrents of water gushing from the ground. It is estimated that the flow from this spring is around 300 gallons each minute.

Lassen Peak

You don't have to be a mountaineer to get to the top of Lassen Peak, for the trail is good and only 3½ miles in length. You climb 2,000 feet from the highway to the summit. Four hours should be ample for the round trip. There are many steam vents and a sapphire crater lake.

From the highest point, you will see clearcut evidences of Lassen's recent activity, also, the distant peaks of the Sierra in the vicinity of Lake Tahoe, the Coast Range ascending northward to the Trinity Alps, and 75 airline miles away the beautiful cone of Mount Shasta.

Lassen In Winter

Lassen is snow country. The fall is so heavy, sometimes as much as 80 feet in a year, that occasionally it is impossible to open the road across the park until the first of July—and even then you may have to drive through snow canyons that reach far above the top of your car. As a result, there is good skiing until fairly late in the season.

The Lassen Park Ski Area is just beyond the southwest entrance station. It is not so large as some, but it attracts many skiers. There is a beginner's tow, an intermediate tow, and a lift; so you will probably find slopes that are just what you want.

No accommodations are open in the park during the winter months, but good facilities are available at Mineral a few miles from the ski area. A sub-concessioner provides ski equipment rental service including boots, skis, and poles. Items such as ski mitts, ski caps, and ski wax are available for purchase. Light refreshments are sold at the snack bar in the winter use building. Ski slope supervision, including first aid, is provided by National Park Rangers and National Ski Patrol members.

LEFT
Bumpass Hell, *one of most important thermal areas in park, presents different picture in winter. Few persons except park personnel see this region during snowy months*

Point Reyes National Seashore

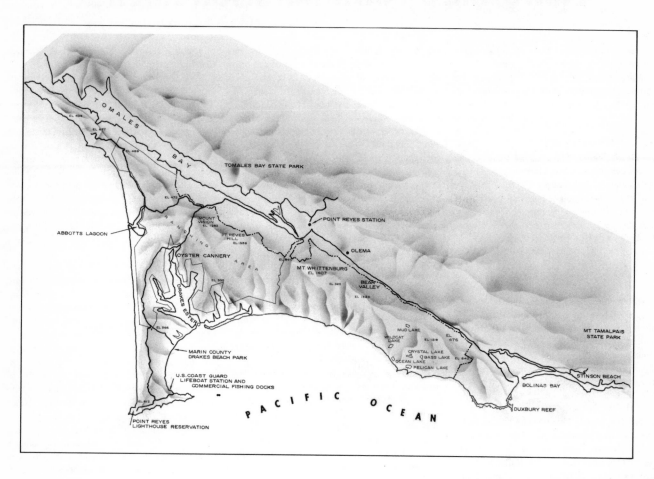

Since early 1963, California has had within its boundaries a national seashore. The newest, and as yet undeveloped, park in the system is Point Reyes National Seashore.

The master package plan has been completed for Point Reyes, and development for public use will proceed as land purchases are made, and funds provided by Congress.

Located on the Marin County coast within 35 miles of San Francisco, and within 100 miles of a total Bay Area population of 5 million, Point Reyes will add a new dimension to the national park system in this state. The first protected national seashore in the state will offer ready accessibility to a range of terrain from long, sandy beaches around Drakes Bay to rugged, wooded highlands on Inverness Ridge. Current proposals call for picnicking, camping, swimming, and boating facilities all around the perimeter from the Bolinas area on the south to the top of Tomales Bay. Much of the interior of this 53,000

acre area will remain in private hands as a cattle grazing range.

Little of the park is at present open to public use. You can now visit the Tomales Bay State Park, the Drakes Beach County Park, and the lighthouse station at Point Reyes. The present system of roads includes 15 miles of Sir Francis Drake Highway (the easiest access, after you turn off U. S. 101 at Greenbrae), some 14 miles of Pierce Point Road, and a 1.5 mile spur road to the county park. The current plans for development call for 25 miles of new roads and improvements on the 40 existing miles, and 25 miles of horse and hiking trails.

The national parks system does not encourage premature exploration of the area, most of which remains in private hands as of this writing. Earliest public use of areas outside the existing state and county parks will probably be no earlier than the summer of 1964.

California's National Monuments

National monuments are areas which have been set aside for their historic, prehistoric, or scientific interest, whereas the majority of the national parks have a primarily scenic value. This characterization, however, is not iron-clad, and there is overlapping. For example, Mesa Verde National Park in Colorado is preserved for its prehistoric cliff dwellings, and Death Valley National Monument has magnificent scenic values; but, in general, the above statement holds true.

California boasts eight national monuments which, in addition to its four national parks, gives the state more than her share of areas administered by the National Park Service.

Death Valley

Everything one hears about Death Valley seems to capture the imagination, and Americans began hearing about it at an early date. The first event to bring Death Valley to attention was the ill-fated 49'er expedition that suffered untold hardships while marooned there attempting to cross it enroute to the gold fields, and it was this party that gave the Valley the name it still bears.

After that, people heard of the twenty-mule teams that hauled out borax. And then there was a mysterious gentleman by the name of Walter Scott, known as "Death Valley Scotty," whose exploits and eccentricities attracted attention to the area. More recently, the Valley has served as the locale for several radio and television series.

But without the 49'ers or Scotty or the mules or television, Death Valley has quite enough to give it national significance. First of all, it is *big*, containing nearly 3,000 square miles of salt flats, shifting sand dunes, great erosional fans, mountains and highly colored formations of fantastic shape. The Valley itself is about 150 miles long and from 4 to 16 miles wide. Flanking it on the east is the Amargosa Range, while on the west the Panamints rise abruptly to culminate in 11,049-foot Telescope Peak.

Some 550 miles of the valley floor are below sea level. One point near Badwater, at −282 feet, is the lowest spot in the Western Hemisphere.

The heat in Death Valley during the summer has not been exaggerated except perhaps facetiously. An old-timer once said that when the lizards crawl under the shade of a creosote bush and turn over on their backs to cool the soles of their feet, it's getting warm—but it's not really hot until they blow on their feet.

Although sometimes the temperature is only about 100 degrees at midday, there are other times when it is 120 degrees in the shade. An official 134 degrees has been recorded, and at Badwater, where no permanent thermometer is located, it may have been hotter. The world's highest official temperature is only 2.4 degrees hotter—reported from El Azizia, Libya.

Death Valley has been tamed from a place of agony and horror encountered by the 49'ers to a comfortable and popular winter resort which thousands seek out each year. From October until May the climate is delightful. The nearer these dates, the warmer the days, but from November until March the average mid-day temperature is between 65 and 75 degrees with average night temperatures from 40 to 50. You can figure that three out of four days will be cloudless and about one in ten will be overcast. Probably you won't have to worry about rain, for the average annual precipitation over the past fifteen years has been just over 2 inches.

Death Valley may be reached from any direction. From the Los Angeles area, it is 282 miles via Mojave and Trona or 306 miles via Barstow and Baker. From the north and west, you can go in through Bakersfield (239 miles over Walker Pass) or down from Reno (372 miles). You can also enter from the east via Las Vegas (140 miles).

To see Death Valley to best advantage, you really should have your own car because it is a large area and distances are long. The highways leading in are good, and the main roads of the monument are surfaced.

There is, however, bus service from Las Vegas. The Las Vegas-Tonopah-Reno Stage Line operates daily except Tuesday, and there is charter service (Tanner Motor Tours or Riddle Scenic Tours). From Barstow or Bakersfield, charter cars are available from Riddle Scenic Tours. Riddle Scenic Tours and Tanner-Gray Line Motor Tours run conducted trips from Los Angeles to the Valley.

If you fly your own plane, you can land on the 5800-foot asphalt runway near Furnace Creek Ranch or an 1,800-foot gravel strip at Stove Pipe Wells Hotel.

During the regular season, October 15 to May 15, you will find a variety of accommodations. The most luxurious is Furnace Creek Inn with its outdoor swimming pool, sun deck, gardens, cocktail lounge, etc. Rates here for two run from $32 to $40 a day, American plan. The pool, tennis courts, and nearby 9-hole golf course are free to registered guests.

About a mile down the road is Furnace Creek Ranch, an oasis in the Valley. Adjoining the resort is a large producing date grove and the golf course mentioned above. The Ranch has a swimming pool, free to registered guests. It also maintains a trailer court with regular hookups. Operated on European plan, sleeping cabins for two run as low as $7.50 and up to $14 with bath. Furnished housekeeping cabins for two are $9.50 up. Meals can be obtained either at the soda fountain or in the main dining room. The Ranch has a spacious, comfortable lobby, as well as a curio shop and general store. Both the Ranch and the Inn are under Fred Harvey Management.

Another popular spot is the Stove Pipe Wells Hotel. This is a comfortable and friendly place operated on the European plan. When you tire of sightseeing you can enjoy shuffleboard, ping-pong, archery, badminton, horseshoes, and croquet. The hotel is an informal place with some 30 cottages and with accommodations for around 135 poeple. Cottage rates for two with bath are $7.50 to $8.50, or you can get a double room in the main building from $9.50 to $10.50. Meals are reasonable and good.

Probably the most interesting place to stay, because of its unique character, is Scotty's Castle which during the past few years has been taking in a limited number of guests. Rates in rooms for two are $6, and meals can be obtained. This isn't a resort as such, but if you want to say that you've spent a night in Death Valley Scotty's Castle, here's your opportunity.

All of the above places are on private land inside the monument and the National Park Service exercises no control over them. The only place operating under government franchise is at Wildrose Station at a higher elevation (and therefore cooler) just inside the boundary on the road from Trona. It is smaller than the others and facilities are not so modern. Cabins and meals are available, and there is also a store and service station.

There is one campground, Texas Spring, in the Valley about a quarter of a mile from the Ranch. It is equipped with flush toilets, tables, and benches. You will have to furnish your own firewood or purchase it at the ranch unless you carry a gasoline stove. Several secondary campgrounds at higher elevations are open for summer use.

As you drive over the main roads in the Valley, you will find most of the points of interest well marked. From these roads, branch spurs lead to features which cannot be seen from the main highway and which you will probably want to visit. Among these are **Mustard Canyon, Artists Drive, Mosaic Canyon, Twenty-Mule Team Canyon,** and the **Old Harmony Borax Works.**

If possible, spend a full day in the northern section of the monument. Be sure to see **Ubehebe Crater** and, of course, **Scotty's Castle.** Take the guided tour ($1.00) through the Castle—it is a trip you will never forget. Take Route 58 outside the monument to the old ghost towns of **Bullfrog** and **Rhyolite** (with its $130,000 railroad station without a railroad), but stop and look back after you have climbed out of the Valley. The view is breath-taking, and this is the best spot from which to see the full sweep of the monument. On the return trip take the one-way **Titus Canyon Road** which cuts to the right before you get to **Daylight Pass.** Consult one of the rangers about the road before you start out, because sometimes it is not in good shape.

In addition to seeing the Valley from the Daylight Pass Road, you should also see it from both rims. Dantes View on the east, at an elevation of 5,475 feet, is a 50-mile round trip from the Inn. Take the road up **Furnace Creek Wash** beyond the Inn. After about 13 miles, the road forks—left to Death Valley Junction and right to **Dantes View.** Another fork to the left a few miles beyond will take you to the abandoned mining buildings at **Ryan.** The buildings are well worth seeing, but the road is steep. When you get to the parking area at Dantes View, you will be directly above Badwater, the lowest spot in the Western Hemisphere. At the parking area, you'll find an exhibit that points out the various features to be seen from there.

You should take a full day for the trip to the west rim of the Valley because there is more to see than the view. Take Route 190 toward Towne's Pass and the left fork at Emigrant Junction. About 10 miles beyond the junction, a secondary road turns left to the old ghost town of **Skidoo.** The road is steep, but you only have to go 5 or 6 miles. The once-popular phrase "23-Skidoo" originated here from the fact that water was brought to Skidoo from a spring on Telescope Peak 23 miles distant.

A couple of miles beyond the turnoff to Skidoo, another road takes you about 5 miles to **Aguerreberry Point,** the best place from which to see the Valley from the west rim. The point is higher than Dantes View (6,279 feet) and probably a better overlook. Six or 8 miles beyond this turnoff is **Wildrose Station.** Take the left fork here and go about 5 miles to the old **Charcoal Kilns.** These enormous beehive-shaped kilns were built in the 1870's to supply charcoal to the nearby mines. Two miles beyond the kilns is the end of the road at **Mahogany Flat** (elevation 8,000 feet).

It *is* possible and even enjoyable to see Death Valley in summer in spite of the extreme heat if certain precautions are taken. Many people cross the Valley enroute east or west, and some visit it just to experience summer conditions. The monument is far from deserted, for the National Park Service staff lives there and there are caretakers at all the resorts. Scotty's Castle and the facilities at Wildrose are open the year around. Gas and oil can be obtained there as well as at Stove Pipe Wells Hotel, which keeps its service station open even though the hotel is closed. The National Park Service has listed certain precautions to be taken by those traveling in Death Valley from May through October. If you follow these few precautions, the chances are that your summer visit will be a high adventure and one which not too many people have had.

1. **Carry plenty of water.** Take no less than 5 gallons extra for your car radiator and ½ gallon for each person. You will find emergency tanks of water for radiators at certain points along the road. Drinking water will stay cooler in water bags or canteens. Don't drink an excess of ice water or iced drinks, and a little table salt in a glass of water several times a day will help greatly.

2. **Be sure to wear a hat in the sun and never go without sunglasses.**

3. **Have enough gasoline and oil.** It is wise to fill up whenever the opportunity offers even though you may not need it.

4. **Don't deflate tires.** The pressure built up by heat doesn't amount to much. Your tires should be in good condition as should your tire tools and jack.

5. **Stay on main roads.** This is very important. Rangers patrol the main roads daily. Unpatrolled roads are so posted.

6. **Don't leave your car in case of trouble.** Wait for a ranger or another traveler to come along even though time drags and you think they'll never come.

7. **Watch your car temperature.** Don't be afraid to shift on hills, thereby reducing the "lugging" of your motor.

8. **Don't get excited, don't take chances, and use common sense.**

Joshua Tree

Similar to Death Valley in some respects, Joshua Tree is vastly different in others. Its 870 square miles embrace hundreds of outcroppings of strangely eroded formations, vast expanses of desert vistas, and above all a rich and varied flora, for here the plants of the Mojave and Colorado deserts meet. There are extensive stands of Joshua trees, members of the lily family that sometimes attain heights of 40 feet, many kinds of cacti with their big showy blossoms, and the lovely ocotillo, and the feathery, plumed nolina. The stately Washingtonia palm is found growing in several of the shady oases on the monument. One grove in **Lost Palm Canyon** contains more than one hundred specimens.

The colorful desert wildflower displays are dependent upon winter rains. The average precipitation here is around 5 inches, and when rainfall is normal or above, the land is a riot of color beginning at the lower elevations sometimes as early as March and progressing to the higher altitudes through June. In dry years, visitors who go just to see the flowers will be disappointed, for the great expanses of bloom will not materialize.

Joshua Tree National Monument is less than 150 miles east of Los Angeles and is rapidly becoming a favorite spot for those who have learned to love the charm and mystery of the desert country. The weather is ideal during most of the year and, although one generally thinks of the desert for winter vacations, summer travel to Joshua Tree is growing steadily. While summers are warm at the lower elevations, one can always seek out cooler campgrounds higher up, for this monument has an altitudinal range of from 1,000 to nearly 6,000 feet in the Little San Bernardino Mountains.

There are no lodging or meal facilities within the monument itself, but there are accommodations in and near the entrance towns of **Twentynine Palms,** where the National Park Service headquarters are located, and **Joshua Tree.** Seven free **campgrounds,** equipped with tables, fireplaces, and toilets, have been developed at various points within the monument, but you must bring your own firewood (or gasoline stove) and water.

There are several "musts" when you go to Joshua Tree. You should first visit the **museum** at Monument Headquarters and take the nature trail through the oasis. By all means go to **Salton View**—the sweeping panorama is one of the finest desert scenes in America. Here, at an altitude of 5,185 feet, you will get the whole sweep of the Coachella Valley with its famous date gardens. To the left, 30 miles away, is the Salton Sea (241 feet below sea level). To the right is the 10,000-foot escarpment of San Jacinto Peak, while farther to the right is San Gorgonio Mountain (11,485 feet), snow-capped during most of the year and the highest peak in southern California. You should see the **Wonderland of Rocks, Lost Horse Valley, Indian Cove, Cottonwood Spring,** and **Pinto Basin.** Joshua Tree is a large monument, and it will take you two or three days of driving to see everything. A good day's circle trip, if you go up the several lateral roads, is from Twentynine Palms through the northern section of the monument to the town of Joshua Tree and back on the main highway outside the boundary. Another trip, which you can take when leaving, is from Twentynine Palms south through the Cottonwood Spring entrance, which will bring you into Highway 60-70 about 20 miles east of Indio.

The roads in the monument are good as desert roads go, but you should stay on the regularly designated ones. It is prudent to carry a supply of water with you, especially in summer.

Cabrillo

Although small in size (about a half acre), this monument has an extremely heavy visitation. Cabrillo is located on the bay about 10 miles from San Diego, and from it one can view what has been described as the finest seascape in the world.

The monument was established to commemorate the discovery of the California coast in 1542 by the Portuguese explorer Cabrillo, who was then in the service of Spain. Unfortunately, the area does not include Ballast Point where the landing is supposed to have been made, but the Point is easily seen from a nearby overlook. An interesting feature of the monument is the old San Diego Lighthouse, originally lighted in 1855 and one of the first to be constructed on the Pacific Coast. There is also an observatory where you can watch at close range the spring and fall migration of whales.

The gate is open from 9 A.M. to 5:30 P.M. daily. There are no facilities for meals, so bring your lunch if you plan to spend the day.

Channel Islands

This is the least visited of any monument in California, since there is no provision for visitors and landings at the present time are made with difficulty. It consists of two rugged islands off the southern coast, Santa Barbara and Anacapa, as well as the waters within one nautical mile of each. The monument was established to protect the large rookeries of sea lions and nesting sea birds as well as the native land and sea plants. Eventually visitor accommodations will be established and the National Park Service will have a permanent representative there, but at present you are strictly on your own with no landing facilities and no fresh drinking water.

Devils Postpile

Situated in the midst of beautiful forest and lake country a few air miles southeast of Yosemite, Devils Postpile is reached from Highway 395 over a 15-mile road, 11 miles of which are narrow and winding but well sur-

faced. The principal feature is a great mass of basaltic columns, one side of which is exposed as a result of glacial erosion. The columns fit together closely like the pipes of an organ and rise in a sheer wall 40 to 60 feet. Most of the columns are vertical, but some are slanting, some are curved, and others seem to radiate out from a common center. You can walk up the unexposed side and stand on a beautifully smoothed mosaic floor where the action of the ice overran and polished the tops of the columns.

The Middle Fork of the San Joaquin River, which flows through the monument, offers fairly good fishing. Walk down the river a couple of miles to beautiful Rainbow Fall, 140 feet high.

There is a ranger station here which is manned during the summer season. A free campground nearby has tables, benches, and toilets. Try the soda water from the springs just south of the campground—take it straight or mix it with lemon juice and sugar. There are no accommodations within the monument, but 2 miles away is **Red Meadows Lodge** where you can get groceries, cabins, and meals. Gas, oil, and a telephone are also available as are pack and saddle horses.

This is a quiet, friendly little monument without too many people. It is at an elevation of 7,600 feet and is always fairly cool.

Pinnacles

Most people prefer spring or fall visits to the Pinnacles, although there is considerable winter travel. The heat discourages summer visits. As the name implies, the area contains rocky spires and crags that rise abruptly over 1,200 feet from the floors of the various canyons. There are several caves, including a rather extensive one through which a main trail passes. This monument is ideal for hiking, for the trails are good (most of them form loops), and they are not too long. There are short easy trips such as the one to the caves area and around **Bear Gulch** and the one from the end of the road on the east side to the beginning of the road on the west. (Ask the rangers about the latter trips.) Then there are other trips which are more strenuous, like the **High Peaks Trail** that opens up beautiful views of the surrounding country, and the trail to **Chalone Peaks**, the highest of which is 3,287 feet and has a fire lookout on top. The trails are varied in their interest, and at one time you may be passing through cool shady nooks with ferns, only to find yourself a minute later on a slope that is hot and dry.

The monument entrance is on the east side and is reached from Hollister or King City. Some road maps, especially the older ones, show a road through the area indicating that

it can be reached from Soledad. However the road from Soledad enters from the west and ends a short distance inside the boundary. Since all development is on the east side you'll have to hike to get there if you take the Soledad road.

There are no meals or lodgings here, but you will find a campground with tables, fireplaces, water, and toilets.

Lava Beds

California's northernmost monument can be visited enroute from Lassen to Crater Lake National Park in Oregon.

Here are fields of lava twisted into grotesque shapes, lava tubes, and cones which resulted from comparatively recent volcanic activity. This is also the site of the main action of the Modoc Indian War of 1872-73. Here, for several months, a small band of ragged Modocs, never numbering more than 71 fighting men, under the command of Captain Jack, held off a greatly superior force of United States troops. This is said to have been one of our country's most costly wars, considering the number of the enemy engaged.

The entrance roads are not too good, but roads inside the monument are surfaced. Other than a **campground**, there are no accommodations, but you can stay at Merrill or at Tule Lake.

You should see the **Indian petroglyphs**, walk through **Captain Jack's Stronghold** (where the Modocs took refuge), visit the museum, and go through some of the lava tubes.

Muir Woods

A short drive over the Golden Gate Bridge from San Francisco will bring you to **Muir Woods**, only area in the National Park System set aside to preserve examples of the Coast redwood, *Sequoia sempervirens*. The monument is small, containing only about 500 acres, but you will enjoy walking over the delightfully shady trail under the trees along Redwood Creek. Since the monument is near the Bay Area, it has a heavy visitation, especially on weekends. The monument is open from sunrise to sunset. There are no accommodations. Lunches and souvenirs can be purchased at the Muir Woods Shop adjacent to Monument Headquarters. There is no picnicking under the trees, but a special picnicking area has been established a short distance from the main gate.

If you don't have a car, you can reach the park by Grayline Tour from San Francisco.